D0170675

Blood in the Sand

Imperial Fantasies, Right-Wing Ambitions, and the Erosion of American Democracy

Stephen Eric Bronner

THE UNIVERSITY PRESS OF KENTUCKY

Scholarly publisher for the Commonwealth, serving Bellarmine University,
Berea College, Centre College of Kentucky, Eastern Kentucky University,
The Filson Historical Society, Georgetown College, Kentucky Historical
Society, Kentucky State University, Morehead State University, Murray State
University, Northern Kentucky University, Transylvania University,
University of Kentucky, University of Louisville, and Western Kentucky
University.

Editorial and Sales Offices: The University Press of Kentucky
663 South Limestone Street, Lexington, Kentucky 40508-4008
www.kentuckypress.com

Maps by Dick Gilbreath at the University of Kentucky
Cartography Labs

09 08 07 06 05   5 4 3 2 1

Library of Congress Cataloging-in-Publication Data
Bronner, Stephen Eric, 1949–
   Blood in the sand : imperial fantasies, right-wing ambitions, and the
erosion of American democracy / Stephen Eric Bronner.
       p.   cm.
   Includes index.
   ISBN 0-8131-2367-4 (hardcover : alk. paper)
   1. United States—Foreign relations—2001– 2. War on Terrorism, 2001–
3. United States—Politics and government—2001– 4. Democracy—United
States. I. Title.
E895.B74 2005
327.73'009'0511—dc22   2005009207

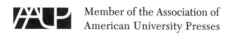

Is this not like a battlefield on which hands, arms, and limbs of all sorts lie strewn amid one another while their spilled life-blood runs into the sand?

—Friedrich Hölderlin

Contents

Acknowledgments

I would like to express my appreciation for the comments and insights provided by my colleagues and comrades at *Logos: A Journal of Modern Society & Culture:* Lawrence Davidson, Irene Gendzier, Philip Green, Kurt Jacobsen, Charles Noble, and Michael Thompson. I also would like to thank Steve Wrinn and Anne Dean Watkins of the University Press of Kentucky for their professionalism as well as their enthusiastic support. Finally, there is my wife, Anne Burns, whose commitment to justice in the Middle East helped inform my own.

Introduction

The Legacy of 9/11—Chronicles of a Dark Time

In the aftermath of September 11, 2001, the day on which the World Trade Center in New York and the Pentagon in Washington were attacked by Islamic terrorists, commentators from virtually every media outlet concurred in the belief that "everything has changed." Few doubted that this event had ripped the fabric of history. Many suggested that the post–September 11 world would prove less innocent, more serious, and more reflective and that significant changes would mark the economic, political, and cultural life of the United States. Insofar as 9/11 created the belief that America was vulnerable to outside attack, that the worst form of antimodern resentment had crystallized in the tragic deaths of 3,000 civilians, and that the "enemy" is not situated in any particular country but rather in a certain region of the world, the symbolic radicalism of the event can hardly be overestimated.

New issues were indeed put on the agenda: "security" against future terrorist attacks became an obsession, a new enemy—an Islamic one—took center stage, "moral values" turned into a slogan, a crude populism gripped the country, and belief in the right to engage in a "preemptive strike" came to define American foreign policy. But although this particular anxiety about an enemy attack on American soil is new, its political translation into a fixation on security and the constriction of civil liberties goes back to the early days of the

Republic. In the same way, although anti-Arab sentiment is, according to Edward Said, "the last legitimate form of prejudice," vilifying an enemy in time of "war" is not new either: America used the image of the "Hun," the "Jap," and the "gook" in other wars in similar ways. Moreover, religion and traditional values usually blossom in periods of crisis; science, progress, and secular truth have never offered much existential comfort. As for vulgar populism, its "know-nothing" excesses constitute what historian Richard Hofstadter termed the "paranoid streak" in American history. It would also be a mistake to think that the new legitimacy accorded to unilateral action and the preemptive strike constitutes a break from the past. Quite the contrary: America has never had much use for the United Nations or for international law and institutions such as the International Court of Justice, and Latin America has been the subject of intervention and coercion since the introduction of the Monroe Doctrine in 1823.

September 11 has not produced a geopolitical transformation of genuine consequence. No remapping of the world has taken place. No alternative to the nation-state has been articulated, and no new and positive response to globalization has been generated. Existing states have not fallen, new ones have not risen, and a number of nations have used the idea of waging a war against terror to advance their own domestic, national aims. What is unique about the aftermath of 9/11 cannot be gleaned from the inflated rhetoric of politicians on both sides of the aisle or from the servile media constantly peeking over their shoulders. Democratic developments have gingerly begun in parts of the Middle East, but they should not be overestimated; nor should the American role in bringing them about. The real legacy of 9/11 can be found in the way that the most reactionary and militaristic tendencies of American history have congealed and been legitimated. Or, to put it another way, since 9/11, economic imbalances of power have become more extreme, political authoritarianism has become more appealing, imperialist ambitions have intensified, and the cultural climate in America has become more constrained than ever before.

To be sure, the events of 9/11 brought out a spirit of unity in the American people. We witnessed police officers, firefighters, and rescue workers risking their lives in the rubble of downtown New York City. America gained a new international standing; its bereaved citizens were accorded sympathy from virtually every corner of the planet. Sadness mixed with fury at the wanton character of the attack. It was unjustifiable in spite of the United States' role in globalization, its imperialist traditions, or its support of Israel and the corrupt monarchy of Saudi Arabia. But the time was still ripe for engaging in what might be termed a "working through of the past." September 11 offered us a chance to clarify why there are some who do not view the United States as the land of liberty. But this brief moment for critical reflection passed. The sense of solidarity, the moral capital accumulated during those terrible days, and the opportunity to reconsider the American project were lost in the first "moment of decision" that marked the new millennium.

What we have now is a symbolically nightmarish event manipulated by an administration composed of consummate liars intent on justifying and reinvigorating the darkest elements and tendencies of the American past. Mired in Iraq as surely as we were once mired in Vietnam, inspired by imperialist ambitions and afflicted by the trauma of a half-remembered military debacle, it might seem that the destruction of cities like Falluja and Mosul was somehow prefigured in the revulsion engendered by the collapse of the World Trade Center on 9/11. But that is not the case. No hidden teleology or determinism produced the quagmire in Iraq or the decline of American standing in the world. Historical or political "necessity," in this case, is just another sound bite. Making this clear, however, requires a willingness to remember things past. That is the purpose of this volume, with its recollections and interpretations of the flash points of foreign policy that led us into these dark times.

Blood in the Sand is intended for a broad popular audience in search of a progressive political orientation. Appealing to such an audience requires writing about complex political issues without jargon, in clear and analytical terms, but with a polemical purpose. Each chapter in this volume responds to a particular moment of crisis or decision. None of them, however, is simply reducible to the context in which it was written. All raise ideas and concerns that point to the future.

Blood in the Sand is more than the sum of its parts. Each of its themes can be understood in terms of a more general attempt to develop the framework for a democratic foreign policy. The volume weaves together issues—and perspectives on issues—that are actually interrelated but are usually treated separately in the current literature. It charts the slippery slope of reaction, beginning when only the whiff of retaliatory violence was in the air and it was still unclear whether the attack of 9/11 should be understood as an act of war, the opening salvo of a more general assault on the West and the American empire, or simply the work of international criminals based in Afghanistan who should be brought to justice.

"Gandhi's Voice" is based on a talk given to commemorate National Gandhi Day of Service at Rutgers University on October 6, 2001, the day before the military bombing of Afghanistan began. Obviously, something grandiose remains about Gandhi's moral legacy. In the aftermath of 9/11, however, his absolute commitment to nonviolence had lost its salience; some degree of retribution seemed a political necessity. Even if it were only a matter of extraditing Osama bin Laden under the auspices of the United Nations, and even if the United States had endorsed the International Court of Justice, military force would have been required. Gandhi's thinking could have proved useful in tempering our emotions, but his absolute insistence on nonviolence needed a corrective. America and the world demanded the exercise of power. For the Left, therefore, it was a matter of insisting upon a plausible—not an absolute, but a plausible—connection between the ends sought and the means employed. The Bush administration was already using 9/11 not simply as a justification for a regime change in Afghanistan but also as the excuse for a far broader undertaking. Thus the warning of my chapter not to beat the drums of war or turn a localized military action into the first phase of an all-out conflict with the Islamic world.

"Us and Them" confronts what soon became the attempt to transform a specific attack on the criminals behind 9/11 into a general imperialist strategy. By manipulating that event and rejecting every opportunity to localize the response, the Bush administration sowed the seeds of the future. Written after the State of the Union speech of January 2002, in which President Bush proclaimed victory despite the failure to capture Osama bin Laden, this chapter explores what would become a new preoccupation with the "axis of evil": North Korea, Iran, and Iraq. These "rogue" states were depicted by the president as the hub of a "terrorist underworld" organized principally in the Middle East, engaged in a transnational conspiracy against the Western democracies, and with access to nuclear and biological weapons of mass destruction. Of singular importance was the way this speech justified the "preemptive strike," the right of the United States to use military force wherever the president believed a terrorist enemy threatened

5

the nation's security, and called on every nation to choose between "us" and "them."

Deepening this division would be accomplished by means of propaganda predicated on the psychological use of projection, hysteria, and exaggeration. The idea that somewhere an enemy was planning a preemptive strike of his own generated hysteria over matters of security that was only intensified by the wild exaggeration of the terrorist threat in the media and by the administration. Little justification was given why the nations constituting the axis of evil posed a greater danger now than in the days before 9/11 or why Saudi Arabia, the homeland of Osama bin Laden and the source of funding for most Islamic terrorism, was missing from that list. But such questions had little resonance. Provisional support for the initial response to 9/11, the assault on Afghanistan, was mendaciously transfigured into an insistence on unconditional support for the invasion of Iraq.

The attack on Baghdad has a personal resonance for me. I was part of a group of about thirty academics and activists who visited Iraq in January 2003, just a few months before the bombing began. "Baghdad Memories" ruminates on that trip, and it recalls our hosts' warnings about what would happen if the United States did invade. We spent time at the half-empty museums and learned much about the theft of cultural treasures by the West; we recognized the importance of not identifying ourselves with either an imperialist invader or a totalitarian victim; and we felt our eyes grow moist while visiting the Al-Ameriya bomb shelter, where 400 women and children were obliterated during the first Gulf War of 1991. We were aghast at the decrepit state of the country under Saddam Hussein and quickly realized that it posed no genuine threat to the United States. We listened with rapt attention as taxi drivers and intellectuals whispered that the fall of Saddam would be welcomed, but a wave of national resistance would engulf any invader.

"American Landscape" illustrates the decline in political discourse that greeted us upon our return from Baghdad. Secretary of State Colin Powell went before the United Nations and falsely insisted that weapons of mass destruction were being stockpiled in Iraq. It is now common knowledge that Iraq had already abandoned its nuclear program in 1991 and its chemical weapons program in 1996. Exiles from Iraq such as Ahmed Chalabi, usually the friends of Defense Department officials, were busily informing the mainstream media that the entire Iraqi populace would celebrate an American invasion. Obviously, it didn't work out that way. Misrepresentation and lying, unfounded accusations and unjustifiable claims, suspicion and hysteria marked the Bush administration's public posture on Iraq. As for the Democratic Party and the intellectual mainstream, little opposition was offered. Crocodile tears about human rights abuses and hand-wringing over national security tended to obscure the genuine interests behind the American invasion of Iraq. Once officials in the Bush administration publicly admitted exaggerating the threat posed by Iraq in order to cement a pro-war consensus, it became apparent that American policy was being driven by the quest for oil, the desire to control water sources in an arid land, the need for military bases in the region outside Saudi Arabia, the prospect of providing a precedent for other nations complicit in the axis of evil, and perhaps an effort to remap the region and shift the military balance further in favor of Israel.

"States of Despair" was written following three weeks of travel in the West Bank during 2004 under the auspices of the Faculty of Israeli-Palestinian Peace. It acknowledges the fact that any strategy for the Middle East ultimately turns on the conflict between Israel and Palestine. More than $4 billion in direct aid and $9 billion in loans are provided to Israel each year by the United States. Resolving this conflict is therefore clearly in the American interest. But few issues generate such emotional intensity, such an inability to see the other side, and such a wealth of myths to justify naked oppression. The situation has grown worse both for Israelis witnessing the decay of the old Zionist vision and for Palestinians experiencing the terrible living conditions in the occupied territories. There have been missed opportunities for peace because of the Israelis' imperialist appetite and the Palestinians' fatal stubbornness, the terrible collective punishments by the former and barbaric suicide bombings by the latter.

So far, the Geneva Initiative is the only serious proposal on the table, even if it lacks official status. Its principal demand is for a two-state solution based on Israeli withdrawal to pre-1967 borders and the creation of a contiguous state in Palestine. But there are problems, including the "wall of separation," the Bantustans of extreme poverty it has produced, the Palestinian insistence on a "right of return," the occupation itself, and the expanding Jewish settlements. Critics of the initiative usually call for a secular binational state, but they have few ideas when it comes to dealing with the intense identity claims, the bureaucratic problems, and the hatred that will surely linger even after official apologies have been made. This chapter offers a different approach though the imbalance of power between the two adversaries makes implementing any lasting solution difficult to conceive. The fall of Saddam Hussein has not changed that.

"Anatomy of a Disaster" highlights what too many still refuse to admit: the invasion of Iraq was less a necessity than a choice justified by little more than imperialist ambition. But it also suggests that the constriction of debate, the creation of a war fever, and the hysteria surrounding security were necessary, in that the American public never would have supported the invasion had its millions of citizens known the truth. All the claims made by the Bush administration have been proved wrong: there were no weapons of mass destruction, there was no palpable threat to the American interest, there was no overwhelming Iraqi support for an invasion, and there was no genuine connection between Saddam and al Qaeda. The invasion of Iraq constitutes the lowest point of American foreign policy since the end of the Vietnam War. But there is something else. The Iraqi war has become tied to a new struggle on the domestic front. Imperialist policies abroad have become linked with an intensification of nationalism and a celebration of militarism that both justify and obscure the constriction of civil liberties and the waging of an economic class war against working people and the poor at home. Too little has been said about how President Bush manipulated the invasion of Iraq to serve his domestic agenda.

The question asked in "Dub'ya's Fellow Travelers," which I wrote in collaboration with Kurt Jacobsen, is: where were those successful academic liberals and moderate social democrats who like to present themselves as public intellectuals, independent thinkers, and gadflys of the established order? They were neither demonstrating in the streets nor exposing the administration's lies. Not all of them supported the war, but none identified with those who opposed it. They were instead rushing to the support of their president. None of them questioned his authority. Intent on defending human rights and extending democracy, without evidencing the least concern for objective constraints or the slightest skepticism about the propaganda they were hearing day and night, these metaphysicians of freedom like to consider themselves "realists." Why even bother noting that the evidence was already there before the first bombs were tossed or that wars are never carried out with the requisite military precision? Some of the fellow travelers started with good intentions; others simply thought that "we" would win and didn't want to miss the boat. Now they are sorry. Some of them say that they were deceived, and others claim that a noble policy was, unfortunately, not carried out to their technical or moral satisfaction. Fellow travelers of times past were legitimately held accountable. That same accountability should be demanded of those mature, responsible, and patriotic liberal fellow travelers of our time who wound up not only endorsing the ideologies underpinning a catastrophic war but—whether intentionally or unintentionally—strengthening perhaps the most reactionary administration in American history.

"Constructing Neoconservatism" analyzes the new rightwing ideology and its political roots. Various leading officials in the Bush administration, mostly but not exclusively located in the Department of Defense, have been quite open about their attachment to the neoconservative cause. Originally brought together in the 1950s through organizations such as the Committee on the Present Danger, the neoconservatives were a group of staunchly anticommunist intellectuals who grossly exaggerated the military threat posed by communism. They still think the same way. Neoconservatives continue to support a foreign policy predicated on a constant demand for increased defense and intelligence spending, an insistence on the right of the United States to intervene unilaterally whenever and wherever it sees fit, and a fundamental preoccupation with the assertion of American hegemony. Important is the way in which each element of the neoconservative worldview intensified a preexisting reactionary tendency and justified that intensification through the memory of 9/11.

Neoconservatism is not simply establishmentarian conservatism writ large; the new worldview is much more radical than its predecessor. In terms of foreign policy, neoconservatives have not merely championed the rape of Iraq but, using the war on terror as a pretext, rehabilitated in more universal terms a paternalistic and imperialistic way of thinking that reaches back to the Monroe Doctrine. In terms of economic policy, neoconservatives—celebrating the capitalism so despised by the 9/11 criminals—have engineered the largest upward income shift in American history, and they remain committed to sacrificing basic welfare and environmental legislation on the altar of a steadily emerging garrison state. Cashing in on the anxieties and nationalism generated by 9/11, neoconservatives are engaged in constricting civil liberties under the guise of security and undermining the spirit of tolerance gained from the social movements of the 1960s. They offer, instead, respect for a new brand of religious fundamentalism and the most provincial understanding of moral values. On the basis of these themes, and a willingness to interpret the legacy of 9/11 in this way, the Republican Party waged its campaign in the 2004 election, and it won.

"It Happened Here" analyzes that electoral outcome and asks: where do we go from here? The Democratic Party raised more money, brought more new voters to the polls, and stood more united in the election of 2004 than at any point in recent history. The Left was crestfallen by its defeat. But there is something to be learned: it is becoming increasingly difficult for a political party to win a national election without mobilizing the base and identifying with an ideological worldview. The Republicans concentrated on mobilizing their base with an explicit ideological message, whereas the Democrats were content to be pragmatic and offer a softer version of what they sought to oppose. The Democrats offered no clear-cut message on the war and no alternative perspective on foreign policy; no genuine assault on the upward redistribution of income and, in spite of their defense of Social Security, no plan for reinvigorating the welfare state; and no coherent ideology other than to support the right to abortion and gay marriage. They refused to confront the structural division between modern-urban and traditional-rural elements of the population.

As usual, the pragmatists and party professionals in the Democratic Party got it wrong. They ignored the political role of ideology in favor of a narrow understanding of economic interests. They didn't consider that the anxieties generated by 9/11 lingered, and they were content to believe that the populace, confronted with an economic downturn, would vote their pocketbooks. It didn't happen. Evangelical fundamentalists and those threatened by the more liberal and cosmopolitan trends of our time voted against their immediate economic interests and in favor of continuing a catastrophic war in Iraq. The country now seems to have been driven even further to the right, and it appears to stand more divided than ever.

The presidential victory of George W. Bush in 2004 bodes ominous economic, political, and ideological developments. Mainstream groups within the Democratic Party, by way of a response, are already insisting on the need for further compromise on "God, gays, and guns." They have little sense of the danger posed by the "new provincialism" and the increasing distortion of democracy endorsed by the Republicans. These Democrats may wish to protect the more elementary gains of the welfare state, but they are unwilling to contest the centralization of intelligence agencies and the new obsession with defense spending generated by the war on terror. They still have nothing unique to say about foreign policy in general, the Middle East, or the logic informing the Iraqi war. These Democrats stand for nothing, and they leave no legacy.

For those on the Left, the issue is not so much salvaging the Democratic Party but rather solidifying a worldview to unite those groups capable of pressuring it from the outside. Only by emphasizing the ideological moment of politics and reappropriating the best progressive traditions of American history—such as the trust-busting of Teddy Roosevelt, the New Deal of FDR, the War on Poverty of LBJ—is it possible to begin reinvigorating public life and the American political discourse. The challenge facing progressives is not merely helping the Democrats win the next election, though such a victory is obviously important, but also re-creating a movement of protest against the erosion of American democracy.

Blood in the Sand can be understood as a democratic intervention into American foreign policy. The realm has traditionally been the preserve of an elite. As globalization continues, however, foreign policy must be increasingly subordinated to democratic norms, and its architects must be held accountable to public scrutiny. A tradition of protest has been growing against the use of the "national interest" to justify the lies associated with the Vietnam War, Iran-contra, and the invasion of Iraq. In contrast, especially since 9/11, a new elite form of hyperrealism, shrouded in the rhetoric of human rights, is maintaining that the United States is divinely endowed with the right to exert its power when it wills. This is a relatively new battle in which leftist intellectuals have a decisive role to play.

Too many public intellectuals of the Left, however, are avoiding the fray. They remain content to indulge their metaphysical inclinations and embrace the need for "balance." In this book's epilogue, "Democracy, Foreign Policy, and War," the concern is with offering criteria in order to aid in making judgments about future actions and further the possibilities of democratic will formation. September 11 has inestimably strengthened the critique of terror. It has also shown the importance of making "secret" information public, openly debating the justification for war, determining what "democratic forces" are in need of help, questioning whether international law is being transgressed, and establishing a plausible connection between ends and means. These are the sorts of issues that should be raised by those concerned with the legacy of 9/11. Only by reflecting on them can dignity be given to those innocent civilians who died so tragically and whose deaths, whatever the slogans of the demagogues, can never be redeemed.

1

Gandhi's Voice

Nonviolence and the Violence of Our Times

I never saw Gandhi. I do not know his language. I never set foot in his country, and yet I feel the same sorrow as if I had lost someone near and dear.
—Leon Blum (1948)

Upon first seeing the image of Gandhi, I received an early taste of racism, Eurocentrism, and cheap cynicism. I remember the cartoon of the mahatma, the great soul, from when I was a child. The Disney Corporation used to depict him as a grotesque, spindly creature with huge glasses and a loincloth looking something like a light brown octopus. Only later, when I entered my teenage years, did I read the short biography *Gandhi: His Life and Message for the World* (1954) by Louis Fischer, which gave me a sense of his true stature: the beatings he withstood, the imprisonments he endured, the kindness and the generosity of his bearing. Over the years I would read many more books about him that stressed his shrewd intelligence and political acumen. His legacy is important when thinking about the United States' response to the attack on the World Trade Center and the Pentagon by the followers of Osama bin Laden.

Many who became intoxicated with the drama of revolutionary violence during the 1960s forgot that the great modern struggle of the colonized for national self-determination began with the emancipation of India under the leadership of Mohandas K. Gandhi (1869–1948). His youth was undistinguished. In England while training for the law, he imitated the styles of the colonizer with little success. Then, following his return to India, he failed in his chosen profession. Only upon moving to South Africa and being tossed out of a first-class train compartment because of his skin color did he become politically engaged. It was in South Africa, where Gandhi remained from 1893 to 1914, and where the young Nelson Mandela later heard him speak, that he developed the doctrine of passive resistance.

The roots of his doctrine were religious: Hinduism, the Bhagavad Gita, and the Sermon on the Mount. Others such as Martin Luther King, Jr. and Mandela would later employ nonviolence to confront rampant discrimination with the liberal rule of law. But none understood *ahimsa,* or "nonharming," in quite so radical a way as Gandhi. He connected nonviolence with *satya,* "truth and love," and *agraha,* or the "discipline of the soul." Thus, in India, a movement emerged that was grounded in *satyagraha*—the personal fused with the political, the individual with the community, religious aims with secular ones—and a new conception of mass action took shape. Satyagraha touched the world in 1930 when, in protest of the despised salt tax imposed by the British, Gandhi and seventy-eight of his coworkers began their famous "march to the sea" in a remarkable display of solidarity among the lowly and the impoverished. Twenty days later, their numbers had swelled to thousands upon thousands, thereby beginning a new phase in the struggle against British colonial rule in the name of an independent India.

Nonviolence was, for Gandhi, both a political tactic and an element in forging a moral way of life. It sought to change the relation between the oppressor and the oppressed. Militant passive disobedience served to instill discipline in its practitioner even as it provided an example of moral rectitude in the face of a brutal enemy. Nonviolence was conceived, in short, as a form of political education. Its aim was not merely to bring about solidarity among the oppressed but also to transform the oppressor. Nonviolence can thus be seen as retaining a universal dimension.

Gandhi was more than the national leader of an independence movement, and he differed from the fundamentalist fanatic who would term members of rival religions "pigs" and "monkeys." Nor did he divide the world into believers and infidels. Gandhi did not dehumanize people; instead, he highlighted the need for a common sense of decency—so lacking today—in political affairs. His notion of *ahimsa* points to the unity of all beings or, in secular terms, what we might consider the harmony between humanity and nature. Gandhi was willing to let a hundred flowers bloom. His life and work provide a sterling rebuke not only to Frantz Fanon and others like him who suggest that violence is the appropriate response to imperialism but also to those inflated realists and hyperrealists who discount the role of ideology and mass-based resistance to what might initially appear to be an overwhelming exercise of power.

Gandhi had his contradictions, as Manfred Steger noted in his fine book *Gandhi's Dilemma* (New York: St. Martin's Press, 2001). The nationalism of his influential journal *Young India* was neither xenophobic nor intolerant. But tension still existed between it and the humanism, the sense of planetary responsibility, advocated by the mahatma. Gandhi also had his weaknesses. He knew little about economics, but his use of the spinning wheel as a symbol of economic self-sufficiency was a stroke of political brilliance. Its immediate practical purpose was to call on Indians to spin their own textiles rather than buy them from the British. But the ultimate value of that symbol—now emblazoned on the Indian flag—was to turn necessity into a virtue. Identifying what is now called "appropriate technology" for an economically underdeveloped India was far less important than putting a positive spin on the economic underdevelopment with which India would obviously be burdened for a long time to come. Gandhi's asceticism, his spiritual purification and renunciation of comfort, similarly had a practical and political dimension: it verged on romanticizing poverty and turning it into what his contemporary, the poet Hugo von Hofmannsthal, called an "inner glow."

Gandhi fused the role of statesman and resistance fighter better than anyone before him. He believed that nonviolence is better than violence but that any form of resistance is better than apathy. Yet he understood that privileging the ethical moment would make his politics more effective. A language of common humanity rather than the inflated rhetoric of self-righteousness and revenge provided his movement with the moral high ground. Ideals were thus placed at the forefront. But he also knew that ideals rigidly divorced from material practice are simply words. Gandhi's greatness derived from the way he connected his principles with his interests and his means with the ends he wished to achieve: equality for people of color and the liberation of India.

The attack on the World Trade Center and the Pentagon offers an example of what Chalmers Johnson has called "blowback," or the unintended consequences of the policies pursued by the United States in the Middle East. The mujahideen received aid from the Carter administration, and Osama bin Laden's subversive activities in Afghanistan against the Soviet Union were supported by President George H. W. Bush. Employing reactionary states and leaders in the "national interest" has been a hallmark of American foreign policy;

sometimes it is necessary and useful—as in the case of the alliance with Stalin in World War II—though usually such realism has ultimately proved counterproductive. It has undermined the United States' standing in the world, especially among the oppressed and exploited, and nowhere more so than in the Middle East, where the cost of uncritical support for Israeli imperialism and a corrupt Saudi regime has been public opinion, or what is known as "the street."

But it would be absurd to place responsibility for this crime against American citizens on the misguided policies of their government rather than on those who committed the act. Seeing the attack on the World Trade Center as simply another occasion to expose American imperialism without privileging the need for a response is an insult to the victims; it is like going to a wake and spitting in the coffin. Simply invoking the oppression suffered by the perpetrators of this action, or those whom the perpetrators claim to represent, doesn't help matters.

Every fascist movement of the past was generated by the experience of real suffering on the part of its mass constituency. Each movement targeted the evils of capitalism, and most castigated the imperialist ambitions of their opponents. The determinate responses to imperialism—not only the indeterminate causes for it—require political evaluation and judgment. Gandhi should help us see that even the victim—and perhaps especially the victim—must deal with the relation between means and ends. Oppression does not justify a politics without aims or even a resistance "by any means necessary." Forgetting that those who perpetrated the 9/11 attack are not our comrades, or simply dismissing the question of punishment and retribution, is both a moral and a political abdication of responsibility.

It may be useful to contrast Gandhi and his followers with the terrorists. Gandhi, King, and Mandela were not only men of peace but also freedom fighters who brought out the best in their people. The means they employed were related to the achievement of realizable ends, and they did not attempt to impose their beliefs on others through coercion. Those whom Richard Falk has appropriately termed "apocalyptic terrorists," by contrast, filled the heads of their followers with the most atavistic and intolerant interpretations of Islam; they killed 3,000 and were willing to kill ten times as many people in their symbolic attack on capitalism. The concrete demands listed by Osama bin Laden concerning Palestine and the withdrawal of American troops from Saudi Arabia and the Middle East, whatever their legitimacy, were relayed after the event. There is no reason to believe that these terrorists would cease and desist even if their demands were met. Osama bin Laden and the Taliban have indicated in word and deed that they despise the most basic values any progressive holds dear and that they are engaged in an ongoing religious assault against modernity and "the great Satan."

"Just-war" doctrine, which dates back to St. Augustine, is a theory particularly susceptible to manipulation. Every war breeds acts of injustice. Even when considering what has been called the "good war," the Second World War, any decent person must shudder at the thought of the devastation of Dresden and Hiroshima. The idea of the "just war" should be turned on its head. War is always unjust and, precisely for this reason, it should always be the tactic of last resort. A moral judgment on whether military action is appropriate depends on an evaluation of the convictions and interests of the enemy no less than the harm done and the threat posed. But it also depends on an evaluation of the convictions and interests of those who are contemplating war against that enemy.

Considering these apocalyptic terrorists as anything more than religious gangsters would be a travesty. There is even something wrong with dignifying their attack as an act of war rather than a spectacular crime. Supporters of the Islamic faith have condemned the terrorists for claiming to speak in their name. These people, too, understand the value of liberty. There should be no misunderstanding: it is a truism that different communities have different customs and beliefs. This does not abrogate the need to make normative judgments about the conflicts between as well as within these diverse communities. The issue here is not religion or some "clash of civilizations"; rather, it is the determination of what is politically acceptable in the pursuit of interests—whether spiritually or materially defined—and what is not.

Terror is unacceptable. That it goes unpunished when undertaken by imperialist states in one set of circumstances does not excuse its employment or justify its tolerance in another set of circumstances. Terror is always totalitarian. It obliterates the difference between guilt and innocence, citizen and soldier; it intensifies the difference between "us" and "them." Terror leaves no room for discourse, and it denies any sense of common humanity or decency. The terrorists who attacked the World Trade Center are totalitarians in Islamic guise; they deserve to be treated the same way as any other totalitarians. Too often in the past, partisans of the Left found ways to excuse or mitigate the severity of terror in the name of "historical necessity" or the suffering of the oppressed. That is no longer possible. History has shown that what is sown in the struggle against oppression is reaped in the new society that is created.

If the just response to oppression is the standard of judgment, then few political figures demand more respect or reverence than Gandhi. We look to Gandhi when determining political actors' responsibility for the tactics they choose and judging their ability to make ethical choices even in the most difficult and immoral environment. But there is a profound difference between Gandhi insisting on the employment of nonviolence by a movement out of power and those today who call only for passivity by a sovereign state whose citizens were attacked without warning. The United States cannot simply ignore the attack of 9/11. Negotiations have been attempted with the aim of bringing the culprits to justice, but they have proved fruitless. Military action looms on the horizon. It would be best, of course, if it was undertaken by the United Nations, and this is a golden opportunity for the United States to endorse the International Court of Justice. But it is important to be clear: even extraditing bin Laden would most likely require the use of force, and the bulk of military hardware and personnel would have to come from the United States. That is the case even though eighty nations, including the Palestinian Authority and various Arab nations, offered support for a military response.

The sympathy extended to the United States and its citizens by the world community is understandable. The assault on the World Trade Center was different from the terror exercised by national liberation organizations in Algeria, Northern Ireland, and even Palestine. There was little doubt in any of these cases that the simple withdrawal of the imperialist aggressor or the introduction of certain policies would end the conflict. But that is not self-evident in the present instance, when the goal has little to do with national self-determination, and religious motivations are paramount. The new terrorists are internationalists, but they are unlike the partisans of the old labor movement. These terrorists demonstrate a commitment to stamping out democracy, and their most secure base of support can be found in the antiliberal branches of an "Islamic Brotherhood" whose influence extends from Algeria and Egypt to Turkey. There is no justification whatsoever for suggesting that a policy of passivity (not passive resistance, because the term employed by Gandhi has no meaning in this context) will mitigate the likelihood of terrorist actions in the future. History also suggests that the strategy of provoking an overreaction is not dependent on any action that the victims of terror might take.

No counterterrorist strategy can ensure the capture of all those responsible for planning and abetting the attack on the World Trade Center. Bombing will not abolish terror, and as the terrorists use noncombatants to shield themselves, civilian casualties will become a growing concern. There is also the possibility that this new "propaganda of the deed" undertaken by the terrorists will ignite a chain reaction of conflict between secular governments and fundamentalist movements throughout the Arab world. Tensions are high in many nations, including Indonesia and Pakistan. Should the latter explode, then India might invade Kashmir, which might result in a war with Pakistan and perhaps even draw China into the conflict.

That there are real risks attendant on military action, however, does not justify applying an old version of the domino theory to the new conditions of terrorism. Bombing by the United States and Britain might not be confined to one nation. That is why political people on the Left should urge a combination of vigilance and caution. It would ultimately be both irresponsible and self-defeating for progressive actors to beat the drums of war or endorse the stirrings of a disquieting new nationalism that harbors its own threats to tolerance and civil liberties in the United States. We must be wary of the rising tide of domestic militarism and the growing preoccupation with enforcing conformity in the name of patriotism. This is a time for uncertainty and provisional decisions

Nothing requires abandoning a critical standpoint. Negotiations with the Taliban, who are shielding bin Laden, must be exhaustive. They must precede any "police action," and if force is employed, the military enterprise should not be equated with a war, let alone a Western crusade, against an enemy without borders, which might inflame billions. Down the road, should any obviously unacceptable consequences result from a widening military action, progressives must be prepared to *quickly* go into the opposition. But then is not now. It is useful to recall what Albert Camus termed the "principle of reasonable culpability." To strike at the bases of the terrorists, to seize the assets of their supporters, and to pressure governments into supporting antiterrorist measures offer at least a chance that the terrorists' activities will be hampered, that a measure of security will be gained, and that a minimum of retribution will be exacted. Perhaps the atavistic and authoritarian Taliban regime will fall; its demise would certainly be no great loss, though what follows might well be victory of the traditional warlords and drug lords rather than democracy.

Gandhi knew that revenge is not politics or justice. There is a real possibility that retaliatory bombing in Afghanistan will turn into the first phase of an all-out conflict with the Islamic world. Under such circumstances, any semblance of a connection between means and ends would be lost. The argument that the end—even the elimination of the terrorist international—justifies the means only begs the question: what justifies the end? There is really only one answer to that: the means used to achieve it. This was the answer Gandhi gave. And he gave it in *absolute* terms. Louis Fischer was correct when he wrote that "Gandhi's means were actually a means to a better means, a better man." The "new man" was an integral part of his political vision. There is even a sense in which the image of the new man lies at the source of all radical action. That vision motivated Mussolini and Hitler as surely as it did

Stalin, Che Guevara, and Mao Tse-tung. But the result was usually less a new man than a new monster. Only Gandhi did not betray the old utopian belief in the new man.

Gandhi remained the mahatma. Purity was the end he sought. But that is not the goal for most who are engaged in politics, and sadly, today we must be a bit more modest in our ambitions. The new man is a mirage, and it is necessary to admit the obvious: a secular rule of ethical conduct must rest on establishing a *plausible,* rather than an *absolute,* connection between means and ends. Those of us on the Left should recognize that in this imperfect world, a perfect symmetry between means and ends is impossible to achieve. And the same can be said of violence. It is what all progressive people hope to mitigate and try to abrogate, even if reality requires surrendering the belief that it can be completely abolished. Gandhi was ultimately right: violence is never a virtue; at best, it is a necessity. Precisely for this reason, to be legitimate, its employment must withstand the most rigorous examination to determine its necessity. The task of progressives thus becomes clear: to hold those willing to employ violence accountable. The most humane and self-evident goal pursued by the mahatma—the abolition of violence—is thus as utopian and as necessary now as it was then. That is the most sobering thought of all.

2

Us and Them

Reflections on Afghanistan, Terrorism, and the Axis of Evil

The State of the Union address offers every president the chance to identify his accomplishments, laud the condition of the country under his reign, and offer a vision for the future. In his speech of January 30, 2002, George W. Bush focused on the need for a drastic military buildup and a new doctrine for fighting terrorism in the aftermath of the attacks on the World Trade Center and the Pentagon by the al Qaeda terrorist network. It would become, arguably, the most important speech of his first term. The picture was painted of a nation at risk since September 11, 2001, imperiled by enemies from without that could strike again without warning. More ominously, Bush insisted, a healthy nation ultimately depended on our willingness to act preemptively in response to the terrorist designs of what he called the "axis of evil"—harking back to the fascist alliance of Germany, Italy, and Japan during the Second World War.

Would that the only issue were Afghanistan. Elections have taken place, but the warlords are still in charge, whether through cabinet appointments or through their private armies, and remain dominant. This first stage in the war against terror was thought to be over even before the invasion of Iraq. Just like in Iraq, however, victory was proclaimed too soon. The Taliban have fallen from power, but they are still waging guerrilla operations from Pakistan, and they have reclaimed control over various parts of the country. Other hopes raised by President Bush have also been dashed. The Afghani economy has collapsed; it is one of the poorest nations in the region. Amid the internecine warfare, the scramble over turf by mullahs and tribal leaders who are little more than gangsters, a democratic future for Afghanistan is anything but a foregone conclusion. Osama bin Laden and much of the top leadership of al Qaeda are still at large. New bases of terrorist operations have formed in Indonesia, Malaysia, and elsewhere. Many thousands of civilians were killed, and following a pattern of carpet bombing, the countryside was devastated. "Collateral damage" in Afghanistan proved greater than expected. But the military action there has already faded. The fighting in Afghanistan lost its importance in the public mind—though it alone was directly and necessarily generated by the assault of 9/11—once a second front was opened in the "war on terror."

America was reeling from the first attack on its mainland since the War of 1812. Sympathy was pouring in from everywhere. Headlines in France read: "We Are All Americans Now!" Public mourning for the victims of 9/11 took place in Germany, Italy, Spain, and elsewhere. There was a legitimate concern that the murderers, along with their defenders, be brought to justice. The American action in Afghanistan was not undertaken in contravention of international law. It was conducted instead with support from the United Nations and the original alliance of eighty nations held firm. The UN was not simply rubber-stamping a decision made by the world hegemon; the legitimacy of the enterprise in Afghanistan was recognized, and for good reason. The charter of the UN does not deny a nation that has suffered an attack the right to self-defense. The link between the Taliban and Osama was crystal clear, negotiations were not being carried on in good faith, and it seemed that a limited action was on the agenda. Only a short time later, the United Nations would oppose the United States over the invasion of Iraq.

Fighting continues in the hinterlands of Afghanistan. But the action there did not turn into a quagmire. Body bags of American soldiers did not swamp the airports. Whatever the inevitable excesses and stupidities associated with armed intervention, millions in terrorist assets were seized and military bases were destroyed. It was also obvious that the U.S. had relatively little to gain in terms of either geopolitical or economic advantage from this attack. Islamic fundamentalism still looms over many states; President Musharraf of Pakistan, the United States' ally in this venture, is himself a military despot; Osama has escaped. Nevertheless, it would seem that some basic objectives of what should be considered a police action have been realized: terrorist activity has been hampered, a measure of resolve has been shown, and a degree of retribution has been exacted in the name of those killed in the attacks of 9/11.

The invasion of Iraq was not a necessary consequence of the attack on the Taliban. Important about the 2002 State of the Union message was the decision to turn the contingent response against a single terrorist attack into a more general war against terrorism. It was a decision that would sever the "war on terror" from the actual events of 9/11 and ignore the real culprits in favor of pursuing a war without end against an enemy without borders. This speech raised the specter of "tens of thousands" of trained terrorists and a "terrorist underworld" organized by Hamas, Hezbollah, the Islamic Jihad, and other supposedly interconnected groups intent on waging a war of planetary dimensions. This speech also initiated what has become an ongoing distortion of evidence, a form of lying with an official imprimatur, which reached its apex with the speech by Secretary of State Colin Powell informing the world about the existence of "weapons of mass destruction" in Iraq. The president emphasized how the victorious troops in Afghanistan had discovered "diagrams of American nuclear power plants and public water facilities, detailed instructions for making chemical weapons, surveillance maps of American cities and thorough descriptions of landmarks in America and throughout the world." This would ultimately be seen as justifying the shift from battling a particular visible enemy clustered in Afghanistan to fighting a transnational conspiracy of "rogue" states and organizations often with little in common. The president noted with pride that the United States had already placed troops in the Philippines and that American ships were patrolling the coast of Africa. But the real focus of the speech was the "axis of evil": North Korea, Iran, and Iraq. Evidence concerning these states' ability to actually employ nuclear and biological weapons remains mixed at best. Nevertheless, the president hammered home that the danger posed by these states was real and immediate.

It is perhaps useful now to make a theoretical detour. Carl Schmitt viewed the distinction between "us" and "them," or "friend" and "enemy," as the organizing principle of politics. This insight by one of the great legal and political theorists of the twentieth century is fairly well known. Somewhat less well known, however, is the implication suggested by Schmitt, a Catholic conservative who wound up being a supporter of Nazism: the stronger the distinction drawn between "us" and "them" by the existing political authority, the more likely the success of its policy. In setting up a situation in which foreign nations must choose to be either "for us or against us," and in demanding what amounts to unconditional loyalty from the American populace, President Bush embraced the logic of Schmitt's argument. His speech heightened the urgency of the present crisis even as it pitted the United States against not only those nations constituting the axis of evil but also those wavering in their will to abolish it. The propagandistic rhetoric was telling, and it would remain so not merely for rallying the citizenry around the invasion of Iraq but also for the type of saber rattling that continues with respect to the other members in the axis of evil.

The propagandistic techniques employed fueled the division between "us" and "them." These techniques consisted of *projection, hysteria,* and *exaggeration.* Imminent threats of attack were projected on states with deservedly poor international reputations but that had nothing to do with the assault on the World Trade Center and the Pentagon. The logic of projection was abundantly clear: an enemy somewhere is secretly preparing to do what the United States is explicitly saying that it will do. Projection thus generated a new sense of hysteria among the American citizenry. Precisely when things began to return to normal, even in New York, terrorist plots were seemingly exposed every few weeks. The *New York Post* wrote of plans uncovered more than a year ago to detonate a nuclear device in the Big Apple. It originally refused to publish the report in order to prevent panic but chose to publish the details in what amounted to a more appropriate time; the report dropped from sight the next day. Other veiled hints of impending catastrophe were used to heighten the sense of insecurity at home; terror alerts were constantly shifting from yellow to orange and sometimes even to red. Especially in the days preceding the invasion of Iraq, when antiwar demonstrations took place all over the world, there was an artificial validation of the original projection and the hysteria it fostered.

The message is that America must be prepared. It is time to revamp our military—and perhaps even our nuclear—strategy with an eye toward the axis of evil. Just as virulent anti-Semitism never required empirical validation of Jewish power, paranoia—or an obsession with national security—can grip a citizenry even when no new terrorist attacks have taken place. It is irrelevant whether North Korea is ideologically disposed toward Islamic fundamentalism, whether the condemnation of Iran has proved disastrous for democratic forces seeking to reform the regime, or whether Iraq had anything to do with 9/11. Forgotten is the once bright possibility for the de-escalation of tensions between North and South Korea sought by President Kim Dae Jung, winner of the 2000 Nobel Peace Prize. Lack of "gratitude" for past support by the United States, rather than serious differences of opinion, supposedly explains European leaders' concerns about the United States' new unilateral foreign policy. That would only make sense. This State of the Union speech by President Bush justified the right of the United States to determine arbitrarily what constitutes a terrorist state or organization and what punishment should be implemented. He stated that his administration had already decided to send 600 "special forces" to the Philippines, 200 to Georgia, and 100 more to Yemen. Steps are being taken to turn the United States back into the policeman of the planet, and this requires fueling the emotional distinction between "us" and "them."

Exaggeration of our peril and the intensification of political paranoia generated by an increasingly conservative mass media are being employed by the Republicans to legitimate the demand for a huge increase in military spending, an increasingly narrow understanding of political bipartisanship, and a foreign policy predicated less on the national interest and more on the president's interest in securing his authority and getting reelected. There should be no mistake. The new antiterrorist effort by President Bush in the year 2002 has nothing in common with the idealistic policy of Woodrow Wilson in 1919. No new institutions like the League of Nations have been envisioned or promised; internationalism is instead subordinated to American unilateralism. For all the talk about extending democracy, which might be an ominous sign, few authoritarian allies of the United States have introduced radical or even meaningful democratic reforms, let alone a democratic form of government. The Bush doctrine has no cosmopolitan vision. It only echoes the vulgar refrains of a provincial jingoism.

There was also something hypocritical in the president's emphasis on "non-negotiable values" such as the rights of women, the importance of free speech, and religious tolerance. It is not as if the Republican Party has ever called for mounting the barricades to further such ideals at home, and considering its "realism" in providing support for certain authoritarian and theocratic allies abroad, talk about "non-negotiable values" turns into little more than a collection of platitudes. By the same token, hardly a word has been wasted in explaining why the danger posed by Iran, Iraq, and North Korea is greater now than it was in the days before September 11. With the exception of nations such as China or Saudi Arabia, not stating what particular measures will be employed against which state and why can similarly be construed less as an oversight than as a way of heightening the arbitrary character of the antiterrorist doctrine, the wiggle room available for its practitioners, and the shifting definitions of "us" and "them."

Mainstream media have not bothered to call for evidence concerning the connections between North Korea and Iran or Iraq, two nations whose relationship has been marked by numerous unresolved tensions stemming from a catastrophic war, let alone those between the axis of evil and real terrorist networks. Its commentators have also studiously ignored the dangers implicit in the new "preemptive strike" doctrine and the way the "war on terror" lacks a clear enemy or even an alliance of enemies, international support, or a general plan for victory. Whether from self-censorship caused by fear or a naiveté inspired by respect for authority, the president is simply taken at his word. Little time is wasted asking whether an elective affinity might exist between the extraordinary popularity gained by President Bush in retaliating for the attack on the World Trade Center and the subsequent attempts to identify his administration with a broader war against terrorism. The terrible tragedy of 2001 has increasingly been manipulated—as surely as the sinking of the *Maine* was manipulated in 1898—to justify a new militarism designed to secure American hegemony in a new global order. What should have been a circumscribed response to a terrorist action is turning into a doctrine justifying American intervention anywhere and anytime.

Terrorism has shown itself to be less a systemic alternative to globalization than a set of scattered responses to it. No remapping of the world is offered, and its "Islamic" strategy, directed against the Western "devil," constitutes no genuine strategy at all. No alternative is offered to the nation-state, though, to be fair, a radically decentralized postmodern organizational vision is tied to a premodern theocratic worldview. Rather than advancing the interests of any Arab state, Islamic terrorism has aggravated tensions between those fundamentalists who support a jihad and more gentle believers who consider the killing of innocent civilians a crime against Islam itself. Western societies can only benefit from exacerbating this tension. But this requires subtlety rather bellicosity. Only the adventurous and militaristic policy of a great power of the Occident against a previously colonized nation in the Orient can produce the xenophobic unification of the split in Islam caused by ultrareligious terrorism.

As things currently stand, existing states have not fallen, new ones have not risen, and a number of nations have used the "international" war against terror to advance their own domestic, national aims. Legitimizing unilateral definitions of terrorism can only lend support to authoritarian regimes in repressing resistance movements. Leaders such as Musharraf have cynically used the antiterror rhetoric to connect their critics with the terrorists. Ariel Sharon has employed it to justify expanding Israeli settlements, and Bush has manipulated it to serve his domestic agenda. In this vein, for all the talk about what divides "us" from "them," little is ever said about what divides "us." Who will pay for an apparently unending war against terror that will increasingly dominate domestic politics? Or, better, what kind of social benefits will be lowered while the private costs of certain groups are raised?

Economic reductionism is unnecessary in noting how the demand for symbolic solidarity against "them" abroad serves as an ideological cover for the pursuit of material inequality for "us" at home. Hundreds of billions of dollars have already been designated for emergency responses in the war against terror, to double the security at our borders and in our airports, and for the development of measures against bioterrorism. The proposed increase in the U.S. military budget is the largest since the Korean War, and it is larger than the entire budget of any other country. Such military increases have been supported by both major parties, and in times of crisis—which it is often in the interest of a sitting president to prolong—neither party is likely to call for reductions. Nevertheless, there is something different going on here: an attempt is being made to place the United States on a permanent war footing.

Always being ready for war and seeking military superiority are staples of political "realism." A new form of "hyperrealism" is being touted, however, given the supposedly inadequate assumptions of more traditional varieties of realism concerning the nation-state as the locus of power, the transient nature of alliances, and calculable interests as the motor of politics. There is some truth to all this. But it would be dangerous to write off the "old realism" too quickly and indulge in a singularly brutal or aggressive power politics without limits. The nation-state remains the point of institutional reference even for transnational movements such as the Islamic Brotherhood. None of these movements, whatever their dreams of an Islamic world, has offered an organizational alternative to the nation-state, and nothing guarantees that they would be successful if they did, even in the regions where they are strongest. The most pressing issue for the United States is probably not recognizing the inconstancy of our Western allies but rather developing criteria, other than a narrow or paranoid understanding of the national interest, for dealing with nondemocratic states or movements. Islamic fundamentalism is not the first ideology that has blinded leaders and followers to their material interests or that has demanded dramatic sacrifices for the cause: communism and fascism came earlier. What should mark this new situation is not simply being realistic in pursuing our interests but—especially in light of a religious and cultural divide—heightening awareness of the connection between interests and principles.

Foreign policy has become more complex in the aftermath of September 11. President Bush has responded by exaggerating an old form of unilateral decision making predicated on an even older form of power politics. Underlying this exaggeration is not some unconscious denial of the new reality but rather a conscious attempt to maximize his ability to deny complexities as he and his administration see fit. The *right* of the United States to engage in preemptive strikes against arbitrarily determined terrorist regimes is being presented as the only alternative to isolationism and a paralytic pacifism. But this argument won't stand on its own merits. The Bush administration is already engaging in a disinformation campaign that will assuredly have salience for future events.

Spontaneous feelings of solidarity are already being transformed into demands for conformity. The range of debate has narrowed, and critics of the antiterrorist war face censure. It is chilling to consider how Tom Daschle, the former Senate majority leader, was castigated by the entire Republican leadership for "dividing the country" and threatening national unity after he finally—if somewhat timidly—suggested the need for a "clearer understanding" of the "direction" informing the present policy. Increasingly, the institutional possibilities for accountability are becoming circumscribed at home, while the implications of the growing asymmetry of power between the United States and both its allies and its enemies are being drawn abroad.

Support for the action undertaken by President Bush against al Qaeda and the Taliban should never have been understood as a blank check. It was provisional, and it should have been articulated as such. Perhaps then there would have been less inclination to juxtapose a "patriotic" Left against a "pacifist" Left. The bitter battles on the Internet that carried over into the debate on the Iraqi war might have been a little less hostile, and disagreement over the issue might not have threatened to produce a permanent fissure among progressive forces. The cry of "irresponsibility" raised by the patriotic Left against the critics of the Bush doctrine has already been stripped of meaning. The moral high ground gained by the United States following 9/11 has eroded. Expectations of solidarity from the rest of the world have turned into expectations of uncritical obedience. Or, more simply, the contingent need for action in a particular circumstance has crystallized into a universal doctrine fueled by the hegemonic ambitions of the United States. These are not developments to be wished for. They are what the Left will have to resist in the dark days ahead.

3

Baghdad Memories

We arrived in the middle of the night, smuggled into Iraq via the Jordanian city of Amman, and the cameras were already waiting. So were the president of Baghdad University, his entourage, some bodyguards, a few agents of the regime, and the organizers of what would become four days of activities in the land of Ali Baba. Half asleep in an empty airport lounge with postmodern arches, some of us talked among ourselves, and others talked with any reporter willing to listen. More than thirty of us constituted U.S. Academicians against War, an independent group of intellectuals from twenty-eight universities and a variety of disciplines. Officially, we were on a "fact-finding" mission, but we realized that a week in Baghdad was not very long and would not turn us into experts. Our real purpose was different: we wanted a glimpse into the society that our government was planning to blast further back into the Stone Age than it had in 1991, and we wanted to offer our solidarity with the Iraqi people, though not the brutal regime of Saddam Hussein.

Holding on to the distinction between the regime and the citizenry, however, meant resisting temptation. We paid our own way, but it was clear that an attempt was being made to seduce us from the moment the motorcade accompanied our bus to an elegant hotel, where we were fed wonderful meals and given more than adequate accommodations. Totalitarian leaders have always liked playing host to visitors who might give them legitimacy. I thought of Aristotle seeking to educate Alexander the Great, Lloyd George and Charles Lindbergh extolling Hitler, and Ernst Bloch and Lion Feuchtwanger pandering to Stalin during the time of the great terror. Every other corner in Baghdad had a poster of the great leader: Saddam smiling benevolently, Saddam with a derby looking respectable, Saddam reading the Koran, Saddam holding a rifle aloft, Saddam with his arm outstretched in a fascist salute. It was important not to become a dupe: I resolved to keep my wits about me and remember what had originally inspired my visit to Baghdad.

Our hotel overlooked the Tigris River. Iraq also possesses the Euphrates as well as the Greater and Lesser Zab rivers. The country once served as a granary, and given the desertlike character of the surrounding area, dominion over this water supply would obviously prove of great importance in any attempt to reconfigure the region. So it occurred to me that, in fact, oil and water can mix. Dreams of controlling these resources surely complemented the desire of the United States to establish a fixed presence in the region. Iraq might also provide a precedent that would show other regimes what is in store for them if they choose to remain recalcitrant when push comes to shove. As we shuttled about, ate our lunch, and smoked the hookah, we sensed that the time was coming when the United States would show the world, once again, who is the boss.

A visit to the Iraqi National Museum gave an indication of who is not. It was pitifully empty, and we saw the impact of cultural imperialism. Obelisks and artifacts from this cradle of civilization now sit in the British Museum and the Metropolitan Museum of Art for the edification of a few dozen connoisseurs and hundreds of bored brats on school tours. The famous Ishtar Gate of Babylon is in Berlin, and the column containing the Code of Hammurabi is in the Louvre. Iraq contents itself with facsimiles as its humiliated citizens recall the glories of Mesopotamia and Ur, the city of Abraham, and the great Arab philosophers Avicenna and Averroës. Better for Saddam to have organized a full-scale legal war to bring these treasures back home—or at least be compensated for them—than to undertake the military adventures that brought his people to the brink of ruin.

And the majority of the country is on the brink of ruin. Other countries might be in worse shape, but it was obvious that, here in Baghdad, things were bad enough. Many of the roads were unpaved, sewage was spilled on the ground, jobless men sat on the corners, and emaciated animals ran through the alleys. We learned that UNICEF had reported a 160 percent increase in child mortality since 1991, arguably the most crucial indicator of public health; this constituted the greatest regression among the 188 nations surveyed. We visited a hospital with rotting walls where children lacked medicines, newborns lacked incubators, and the doctors treated 150 patients a day. Then we were taken to the Al-Ameriya bomb shelter, where 400 women and children lost their lives in 1991. It was a stark underground casket preserved as a museum; we could still see the twisted iron, the remains of bodies plastered against the walls, the victims' blood on the floor and ceiling. The United States still claims that the bombing of this shelter, which lies in a residential area, was a mistake. But that doesn't help the victims. This monument remains etched in my mind; it embodies the face of war and what these poor people will most likely have to endure again.

Saddam's Iraq was not built on a war economy. Its infrastructure was shot; it did not have the grandiose imperialist and racist ideology of the Nazis; it was not even potentially the dominant power in the region. Nor was the situation akin to that of Hitler during the 1930s, when the famous policy of "appeasement" was applied. A better historical analogy can be found in the period immediately following World War I. Just as the Treaty of Versailles insisted that Germany admit its "war guilt" and pay enormous reparations, if a war should take place, Iraq will be forced to take responsibility for its own destruction while oil profits are used to compensate the United States. The Treaty of Versailles generated a new nationalism in Germany that undermined the Weimar Republic and fueled the Nazi movement. Based on our conversations with Iraqis, it was easy to imagine a postwar Iraq convulsed by ethnic groups with irredentist longings, unified by a hatred of the West and contempt for what will surely become an American puppet regime.

The United States will assuredly not relinquish control. Iraq might, however, be carved up into three rump states. Turkey has its eye on the Kurdish areas in the north, and it has received more than $25 billion in loans and aid as compensation for the stationing of American troops. Iran has designs on a Shiite protectorate along its border. The potential for conflict between these two nations is real, and the Sunnis are inflamed by nationalist yearnings of their own. There is, in principle, no need for Iraq to exist within its present borders, which were artificially created by long-gone imperialists.

If Saddam and his henchmen can be ousted without devastating the country, creating a maelstrom in the region, causing an extraordinary loss of life, and totally perverting the international rule of law, then so much the better. But that seems unlikely. It has been estimated that in the first forty-eight hours, 800 bombs will fall on Baghdad and 3,000 on Iraq; genocide could result from what has been termed a policy of "shock and awe." An internal memorandum from the United

Nations estimating the costs of the war projected nearly a million refugees, hundreds of thousands of casualties, destruction of the infrastructure, and a proliferation of diseases. The impact on the economy of the region could also prove devastating. There is even the danger of nuclear war. Military spending and the costs of an American occupation could reach into the hundreds of billions of dollars. As for humanitarian aid, President Bush initially deemed $15 million sufficient. The casual way in which George Bush and Tony Blair gambled with the fate of an entire region and its inhabitants is unreasonable and imprudent, morally unconscionable, and politically reckless. Opposition to the policies of the warmongers will be justified even if they win their bet.

The foreign policy of the Bush administration has been a disaster from the beginning. Its architects have isolated the United States from the world community by refusing to endorse the modest environmental reforms of the Kyoto Protocols, declining to make Americans subject to the International Criminal Court, and rejecting the Anti-Ballistic Missile Treaty. Negotiations with North Korea have given way to nuclear saber rattling. The United States is experiencing the deepest rift with its erstwhile allies France and Germany since World War II. NATO is virtually paralyzed on the matter of defending Turkey in case of an Iraqi invasion. Any pretense of balance in the Middle East has disappeared as the United States has issued a virtual carte blanche to Ariel Sharon in his bloody war against the Palestinians. In its relations with the UN, the United States has acted like the bully in the schoolyard who throws a temper tantrum when a call goes against him. The sympathy gained in the aftermath of 9/11 has been squandered. The world is clearly appalled that the United States (the only nation ever to employ nuclear weapons) has expressed its readiness to fight unilaterally and is demanding the certain devastation of Iraq for flaunting international resolutions pushed through by the United States because its enemy *might* develop and then *might* employ nuclear weapons sometime in the future.

There is little reason to believe that the present policy will make the Western world more secure against terrorism. The Al-Kadhimain Mosque, the largest mosque in Baghdad, is beautifully ornate, with a golden dome. We found it packed on a weeknight; just a few years ago, we were told, it would have been empty. The bellicosity of the Bush administration is fueling the fires of fundamentalism and undermining the position of Western-style liberals in the region. If Saddam really does have chemical and biological weapons, which everyone doubts, then engaging in a war to the death will create the greatest incentive for Iraq to deploy them. A boomerang effect, blowback, or whatever one calls it looms on the horizon. The present policy is in danger of bringing about precisely what it most seeks to avoid.

Saddam is a thug whose treatment of the Shiite majority and the Kurds was ruthless and brutal. But the United States was willing to do business with him in better times, just as it was willing to deal with Batista in Cuba, Diem in South Vietnam, Pinochet in Chile, and Somoza in Nicaragua. It always seems to be a matter of deciding whether the dictator in question is, using FDR's phrase, "our son of a bitch" or not. The regimes themselves were not remarkably dissimilar. The character of Saddam's Iraq became clear to us as we listened to a kindergarten class sing a hymn in praise of him, a group of children with Down syndrome plead for peace, and—far worse—certain of his party loyalists present a set of academic papers that made it abundantly clear how the authoritarian climate dulls meaningful discourse and casts a shadow over public life. No hint of criticism was ever openly expressed.

Anti-Semitism of the old sort also cropped up in any number of conversations. Even intellectuals referred to the existence of a Jewish conspiracy explained by the infamous fabrication of the Russian secret police known as the *Protocols of the Elders of Zion*. Few knew about the Israeli opposition or even Peace Now. Just as the mainstream media in the United States identified Iraqi nationalism with Saddam Hussein, so have the Iraqi media identified the interests of all Jews with Ariel Sharon.

Intelligent policies can't be built on stupid assumptions. The self-defeating character of such censorship and propaganda was obvious. New friends we met in private admitted as much. They were aware of their intellectual isolation. They criticized the militarism of the regime. They called for international organizations to monitor civil liberties. They knew what they were dealing with. But some of the best people in our party—a number were inspired by the Christian belief in good works and bearing witness—must have encountered different people with different views. They felt that it was not our place to judge the Iraqi state and believed that criticism would only undermine the antiwar effort. Others, including myself, disagreed. We argued, but we never lost our sense of common purpose. We never forgot the warmth with which so many ordinary Iraqis greeted us. They were grateful for our visit and terrified by the thought of another war.

In my opinion, the final statement by our group (reproduced at the end of this chapter) should have been more critical of Saddam's regime for its exploitation of the misery caused by the sanctions, its corruption, its foolhardy militarism, and its assault on human rights. Ultimately, however, we were in Baghdad to show our solidarity with the citizenry and to foster opposition to a looming war led by the United States. We agreed on the need to clarify the regional implications and secondary effects that might result from the current policy and to insist on ending sanctions on nonmilitary goods and improving relations between the two countries. All of us were appalled at the thought of a "preemptive strike" and disgusted by a peculiarly American arrogance in the conduct of foreign affairs that reaches back to the Monroe Doctrine of 1823.

During the long plane ride home, wondering how we would be received, I became angry thinking about our ever-narrowing national discourse, the shrill dogmatism of media pundits, our disregard for international law, the arrogance of the Republicans, and the cowardice of the Democrats. We were returning to a country with a huge new agency for "homeland security," new constrictions on civil liberties, and a mainstream debate that ranged from those ready to bomb Iraq right now to those willing to wait a few months before doing the same thing. "America! Love it or leave it!" and "My country! Right or wrong, my country!" I remembered such slogans from the time of the Vietnam War. But who were the real traitors: those who insisted on continuing to send young people to die in a hopeless war, or those who sought to end that war?

A simple UN resolution would not make an attack on Iraq more palatable; the dangers and the costs would remain the same. Just as a patriot does not have to agree with every action undertaken by the United States, an internationalist does not have to support every action undertaken by the United Nations. Neither genuine patriotism nor genuine internationalism requires one to be a toady or an idiot. Criticism cannot be seen as precluding positive convictions. The words used by the libertarian socialist Rosa Luxemburg in castigating Lenin and Trotsky in 1918 retain their validity today: "Freedom only for the supporters of the government is no freedom at all. . . . Freedom is only and exclusively freedom for the one who thinks differently."

As we landed, I thought of the Gulf War of 1991. I suddenly realized that every person I had met in Iraq—the television reporter who had lost her niece, the law professor who had lost her aunt and cousin, the handsome taxi driver who had lost some fingers, and the veterinarian who had lost his house—might be dead in a matter of weeks. If nothing else, this trip allowed me to put a face on the victim and gain a deeper understanding of what we so blithely term "collateral damage." I thought of those young people, not so different from those in my classes, who might also lose their lives in this war. All the members of our group, I think, were inspired not merely by humanitarian motives but also by the genuine interests of the United States. We did what we could. Perhaps we were naive. But we also knew that if this war were averted, it would be because naive people around the world had risen up in protest. It would be because they insisted on peace rather than war and proved willing, in the famous phrase, "to speak truth to power."

Statement of the Delegation of Independent United States Academics to the Iraqi-American Academic Symposium, University of Baghdad, January 14–16, 2003

We are a diverse group of independent academics—faculty, staff, and students—from twenty-eight universities, twenty-one states across the United States, and a range of disciplinary fields—archaeology, astronomy, communications, computer science, conflict resolution, environmental studies, geography, history, law, leadership studies, mathematics, medicine, Middle East studies, nursing, peace studies, philosophy, political science, psychology, public health, religious studies, social work, and sociology. We are not apologists for any nation or government.

Although we reflect a wide range of views on many domestic and international issues, we find ourselves united in our opposition to United States policies regarding Iraq. We brought with us a hope for peace and the beliefs that no accepted doctrine of international law, nothing in the United Nations Charter or any UN resolution, and nothing in the law and tradition of the United States authorizes or warrants the government's threatened preemptive attack on Iraq or its pressure on the United Nations to condone such an attack. Finally, we believe that the vast financial expenditures necessary to support this ill-advised military venture would divert much-needed resources from urgent domestic priorities facing Americans at home.

We traveled to Iraq to see for ourselves, insofar as possible, the conditions prevailing in that country. We found that UN sanctions and their international and local administration have already had a devastating effect on the civilian population. Further, the human and ecological impact produced by an attack on Iraq would be catastrophic. We also came to understand better the likelihood that tensions in the Middle East would grow, militant fundamentalism would increase, and the moral standing of the United States would deteriorate. We also came to understand the serious inadequacy of most media coverage in the United States by its almost exclusive focus on Iraq's leader. This proposed war would cause needless further death, injury, and hardship to the 24 million citizens of Iraq, to American soldiers placed in harm's way, and to those innocents in the United States, Israel, and elsewhere who would be victimized by retaliatory actions. Furthermore, the destabilizing effect on global security and the prospect of nuclear war cannot be dismissed.

For these reasons, we:

1. Implore the United Nations and its constituent members to oppose the United States government's threatened preemptive attack;

2. Urge the United Nations to lift all sanctions that have harmful consequences: for the young, the sick, and the dying, who cannot receive adequate medical treatment; for farmers who cannot farm their land without needed equipment; for the many ordinary Iraqi citizens who are still left without clean water supplies and sanitation; and for students and scholars for whom free inquiry and education have been curtailed even though they provide the surest path to human rights and civil liberties;

3. Implore the United States government, as a permanent mem-

ber of the United Nations Security Council and as a preeminent world power, to fulfill its proper leadership role by cooperating on the international stage and complying with international law;

4. Urge both nations to pledge to protect and expand academic freedom, and to strengthen cultural understanding through increased exchanges between faculty, students, and other citizens;

5. Urge both governments to take every opportunity to engage in a direct diplomatic dialogue to reduce their mutual sense of threat; and

6. Call upon our 33,000 academic colleagues, who, like us, signed the No Iraq Attack petition (www.noiraqattack.org), to conduct seminars and forums on their campuses advocating the points above; to work for exchanges of faculty and students on their campuses with the universities of Iraq; and to join networks to support the faculty and students of Iraq with teaching and scholarly materials.

There is still time to avoid war.

4

American Landscape

Lies, Fears, and the Distortion of Democracy

In memory of my student Rute Moleiro

Lying has always been part of politics. Traditionally, however, the lie was seen as a necessary evil that those in power should keep from their subjects. Even totalitarians tried to hide the brutal truths on which their regimes rested. This disparity gave critics and reformers their sense of purpose: to illuminate for citizens the difference between the way the world appeared and the way it actually functioned. Following the proclamation of victory in the Iraqi war, however, that sense of purpose became imperiled, along with the trust necessary for maintaining a democratic discourse. The Bush administration boldly proclaimed the legitimacy of the lie, the irrelevance of trust, and the mainstream media essentially looked the other way.

Not since the days of Senator Joseph McCarthy has such purposeful misrepresentation, such blatant lying, so dramatically tainted the American landscape. It has now become clear to all except the most stubborn that justification for the war against Iraq was based not on "mistaken" interpretations or "false data" but on sheer mendacity. Current discussions among politicians and investigators focus almost exclusively on the false assertion contained in sixteen words of a presidential speech to the effect that Saddam sought to buy uranium for his weapons of mass destruction in Africa. The forest has already been lost for the trees. We are told that the problem derived from faulty intelligence by subordinates rather than purposeful lying by those in authority. CIA officials, however, have openly stated that they were pressured to make their research results support governmental policy. Secretary of State Colin Powell has still not substantiated claims concerning the existence of weapons of mass destruction that he made in his famous speech to the United Nations. Doing so would be difficult. The chief American inspector for Iraq, Charles A. Duelfer, has offered a report and testified before Congress that, under pressure from the United Nations, Iraq ended its nuclear program in 1991 and closed down its last biochemical weapons plant in 1996; he also found no evidence of an attempt to restart those programs (*New York Times*, October 7, 2004).

But then various members of the Bush inner circle cheerfully admitted that the threat posed by Iraq had been grossly exaggerated. No matter: hyping the threat was useful in building a consensus for war. The Bush administration itself nonchalantly verified what critics always knew: that American policy was propelled by greedy thoughts of an oil-rich Iraqi nation, the desire to control four rivers in an arid region, the opportunity to throw the fear of the Western God into Tehran and Damascus, and the chance to establish an alternative to the military presence that once existed in Saudi Arabia. Wrong on every count in Iraq—the existence of weapons of mass destruction, the threat posed by the decrepit dictatorship, the degree of popular support for American intervention, and the degree of possible resistance—the CIA was either incompetent beyond all reason or, more likely, served to protect the president from domestic criticism by acting as what Thomas Powers called a "foreign ministry of spin." Former director of the CIA George Tenet ultimately took the fall. But the Bush administration has chastised none of the principal advisers who championed its catastrophic policy in Iraq, even as attacks by the Democratic Party with respect to the war and its conduct were qualified to the point of insignificance.

"Leaders" of the so-called opposition party cowered in their offices. They obviously feared being branded disloyal. As they quaked in their boots and wrung their hands, they had little time for issues pertinent to the national interest. It was not their fault that debate over the broader justification of the war had been steadily disappearing from the widely read right-wing tabloids such as the *New York Post* and, at best, retreating to the middle pages of more credible newspapers. Elected politicians in both parties, scurrying for cover, routinely made sure to note that their support for the war did not rest on the existence of weapons of mass destruction in Iraq. Few considered it necessary to mention that the lack of such weapons, combined with the inability to find any proof of a link between Saddam Hussein and al Qaeda, invalidated the claim that Iraq posed a national security threat to the United States. Everyone in the political establishment now points to humanitarian motives. For the most part, however, such concerns were not uppermost in the minds of those occupying the "war room" of the White House *then,* and there is little reason to believe that they consider them decisive now. Human rights became important for self-styled "realists" such as Paul Wolfowitz and Richard Perle only when claims concerning the imperiled national interests of the United States were revealed to be vacuous.

President Bush and members of his cabinet no longer bother to insist that the weapons will ultimately be found or that links to al Qaeda will soon be unveiled. This acknowledges that the evidence did not exist when the propaganda machine initially began to roll out its arguments for war. The administration had untold intellectual resources from which to learn that the United States would not be welcomed as the liberator of Iraq and that serious problems would plague the postwar reconstruction. But it wasn't interested. Decision makers within the administration remained content to forward a position and then find information to back it up. This begs two obvious questions: Would the American public have supported a war against Iraq had they known the truth? And perhaps more importantly, did this self-induced ignorance about conditions in Iraq help produce the current morass in which billions of dollars have been wasted and every day more American soldiers are injured or killed?

Millions of dollars were spent by a special prosecutor investigating false allegations of financial impropriety by Bill and Hillary Clinton. Impeachment proceedings were begun following the revelation of an affair between President Clinton and an intern. The media were up in arms. Many still pat themselves on the back for their role in bringing about the Watergate hearings. But when it comes to the chorus of untruth perpetrated over the invasion of Iraq, which has already cost more than 1,700 American and—according to the Lancet Website—100,000 Iraqi lives and billions of dollars, the public interest is apparently best served by "bipartisan" committees and a press corps scared of its own shadow. Just as the Republican Party was flagrant in its refusal to rationally justify its war of "liberation," the Democratic Party seemed less concerned with self-criticism and its inability to offer a principled alternative stance on foreign policy than with the Far Left—led by the erstwhile supporters of Governor Howard Dean (D-Vt.)—taking over its party apparatus.

Important members of the Democratic Leadership Council poignantly asked during the primaries whether the party wishes "to vent or govern," and when questioned about its current disarray, Senator Birch Bayh of Indiana, chairman of the organization, was quick to blame the antiwar critics by responding that it was a matter of "assisted suicide." He and the rest of his comrades talk big about the failings of the Left. But their tone changes when it comes to their feeble efforts to define their message and their willingness to swallow whatever the Bush administration puts on their plates. Democrats were quick to use leaks from the intelligence community, many of whose members were aghast at the misuse of their research, to condemn the Bush administration. But they were never able to explain how they or their staffers ignored the flood of disbelief on the Internet concerning supposed links between Saddam and al Qaeda, the existence of a nuclear program, and the idea that Iraq posed a threat to the United States. Their credulity in the face of the propaganda blitz, or their cynical cowardice in refusing to stand against it, makes these Democrats almost as culpable as the Republicans for what transpired.

The mainstream "opposition" still has not acknowledged that it was bamboozled or that the war was a disaster from the beginning. Unable to admit their complicity in bringing the war about and their lack of either nerve or a critical sensibility, the "responsible," "moderate," and—above all—"patriotic" leaders of the Democratic Party always speak the language of pragmatism and moderation. Unfortunately, however, their pragmatism is anything but pragmatic. They conveniently forget the congressional election of November 2002. By all serious accounts, it was their inability to offer any meaningful alternative to the policies of President Bush that led to the worst nonpresidential-year losses in American history. It also apparently doesn't matter to them that the American public has never embraced "bipartisan" candidates like Joseph Lieberman. Unwilling to take a stand on principle, since it *might* cost them some votes, they don't seem to mind that being a little less right wing than the Republicans on tax cuts, social welfare, and the war is undermining any genuine loyalty to a party that once identified with FDR, Bobby Kennedy, and Paul Wellstone. Senator Bayh and his friends haven't a clue: the Democratic Party can neither vent *nor* govern. Democrats should worry about their image—especially since they don't have one.

The United States appears less like a functioning democracy in which ideologically distinct parties and groups debate the issues of the day and more like a one-party state ruled by shifting administrative factions. Free speech exists, but having a formal right and making substantive use of it are very different matters. Consensus and bipartisanship are becoming increasingly paranoid preoccupations of the media and party professionals, whose range of debate extends from humpty to dumpty. Noam Chomsky may not be everyone's taste, but his little collection of interviews *9/11* (Seven Stories Press) was *the* best-selling work on that terrible event. When was the last time you saw him interviewed by the mainstream media?

It is the same with Frances Fox Piven and any number of other radical or progressive public figures. Every now and then, of course, Cornel West may pop up for an interview on MSNBC. Robert Scheer continues to write for the *Los Angeles Times* and Paul Krugman for the *New York Times.* Sean Penn can still pay for a full-page advertisement to express his critical views on the war. A few genuinely progressive politicians such as Barbara Lee (D-Calif.), Sherrod Brown (D-Ohio), and Lynn Woolsey (D-Calif.) will occasionally speak their minds. In fact—though only after the emergence of a groundswell from below—even former vice president Al Gore challenged the veracity of the Bush administration.

But their voices certainly don't dominate what conservatives and right-wing pundits—always ready to view themselves as victims of the system they control—castigate as the "liberal" media. Career talking heads usually just nod and counsel prudence. Most of them are taught to be careful. They know how the game is played, and they hedge their bets. So long as some element of a statement made by the president is technically true, the boss will be let off the hook. Others are in the pocket of the administration, a few are bribed, and eyes are closed all around when it comes to the use of staged photographs and faked interviews. The false justifications for what can only be considered one of the major blunders of American foreign policy in the past century were ultimately treated—or, better, "interpreted"—with the same degree of esoteric obscurantism as a complex business contract or a convoluted literary text.

This revolting display by the mainstream media brings to mind the vision of a society dominated by what Herbert Marcuse termed "repressive tolerance"—a world in which establishmentarians can point to the rare moment of radical criticism to better enjoy the reign of an overwhelming conformity. The evidence is everywhere. CNN is only a minor player when compared with the combined power of television news shows with huge audiences hosted by mega-celebrities such as Rush Limbaugh, Bill O'Reilly, and Pat Robertson. Belief in the reactionary character of the American public has generated a self-fulfilling prophecy: the public gets the shows it wants, which in turn only strengthen the original prejudices. Edward R. Murrow, so courageous in his resistance to the hysteria of the 1950s, is often invoked by the fourth estate, but that invocation is merely symbolic.

Hardly a word is said about the skepticism of the millions who participated in the mass demonstrations or how criticism by the mainstream affected Tony Blair and the English political landscape. Neither the intensity of the criticism nor the bravery of the critics was matched in the United States during the early days of the conflict. More than fifty former officials of the English foreign affairs ministry castigated Blair's decision to support the United States in its invasion of Iraq. Indeed, according to the *Independent* of June 18, 2003, the former secretary of state for international development, Clare Short, and the former foreign secretary, Robin Cook, publicly insisted that "half truths, exaggerations, and reassurances that were not the case" were employed, along with "selective intelligence," to produce the "honorable deception" required to lead England into a shameful war.

One criterion for judging democracy is the plurality of views presented to the public; the number of views expressed usually reflects the number of political options from which the public can choose. A chill is passing over America. It is striking to reflect on the range of debate during the Progressive Era, the New Deal, and the 1960s. Even so, governmental attempts to constrict civil liberties in moments of crisis have been a fundamental trend of American history. But this trend is currently being celebrated in a new way and with new force. It is sobering to consider how debate over the legitimacy of a terrible war has been narrowed—with the acquiescence of most establishmentarian critics—to sixteen words in a presidential speech and an increasingly corrupt evaluation of policy options.

It is no wonder that the American public has proved itself increasingly incapable of grasping how much distrust its government inspires elsewhere. A current Pew poll of more than forty-four countries, directed by former secretary of state Madeleine Albright, shows that distrust of the United States has grown in an exceptionally dramatic fashion in each of them. This includes sensitive nations such as Pakistan, Saudi Arabia, Turkey, and Indonesia, where unfavorable ratings of the United States have gone from 36 percent in the summer of 2002 to 83 percent in May 2003. And this only makes sense: the paternalism with which the will of the world was treated by this administration, coupled with its mixture of bluster and mendacity, is unprecedented.

The "streets" of Europe and, more importantly, the Arab world have been lost. Perhaps they will be regained at a future time. But the numbers in this poll express anger at a basic reality. Trust and loyalty cannot be commanded by military power. With its new strategy of the "preemptive strike" buttressed by a $420 billion defense budget, bigger than that of eighteen of the most "well-defended" nations put together, the United States has rendered illusory the idea of a "multipolar world." It has become the hegemon amid a world of subaltern states, and it has no need to listen or debate. The difference between truth and falsehood no longer matters. There remains only the fact of victory, the fall of Saddam Hussein, and the bloated self-justifications attendant on what Senator J. William Fulbright, the great critic of the Vietnam War, termed "the arrogance of power."

Americans have traditionally tended to rally around the president in times of war. Fulbright himself accepted President Johnson's claim that an American military vessel had been attacked in the Gulf of Tonkin and, in 1964, voted in the Senate for a decision that would ultimately be used to bolster the U.S. role in Vietnam. When asked about his decision later, Fulbright supposedly replied, "Was I supposed to call the President of the United States a liar?" That would have been almost unprecedented at the time, and it would have been hard to expect from a senator. But then is not now. The "liberals" in the Democratic Party really should have learned something from the conduct of presidents during the Vietnam War, Watergate, and Iran-contra. It would be sad if they didn't, since this war against terror is not like other wars. President Bush has admitted that it has no end in sight. The question is: how much rope will "responsible" liberals give before he hangs them?

A new department of "homeland security" has been created, and the civil liberties of citizens are imperiled. Justification is supplied by manipulative and self-serving "national security alerts" in which the designation of danger shifts from yellow to orange to red and then back again without the disclosure of any evidence regarding why a certain color was chosen and why it was changed. The "bully pulpit" of the president, as Theodore Roosevelt called it, can go a long way in defining the style of national discourse and a sense of what is acceptable to its citizenry. This is where leadership asserts itself; the Democrats can go home now. Nevertheless, it is precisely on this question of leadership, for which President Bush has received such lavish praise, where he is weakest.

Beyond all social policy concerns or disagreements over issues of foreign policy, this president is presiding over a newly emerging culture in which truth is subordinate to power, reason is the preserve of academics, paranoia is hyped, and know-nothing nationalism is celebrated. No longer is the constructive criticism of genuine democratic allies taken seriously; better to rely on a corrupt "coalition of the willing" whose regimes have been bribed, whose economies have been threatened, and whose soldiers have been exempt from fighting this unending war on terror. The opportunity for self-reflection has been missed, no dialogue over the decline of American standing in the world has taken place, and there has been no hint of an apology by the Bush administration for its conduct in the weeks before the war broke out. In 2001, Donald Rumsfeld closed down the short-lived Office of Strategic Influence, lodged in the Pentagon, which covertly fed propaganda and misinformation to the media to shape opinion in enemy and neutral nations; now, apparently, its approach is being resurrected to meet American needs in the Middle East. That such false information will find its way back home is only logical. The question, then, for the American public, and for the citizens of other nations, is this: how can one trust a liar whose arrogance is such that he finds it unnecessary to conceal the lie?

Democracy remains elusive in Iraq, Afghanistan is languishing in misery, and new threats to the national security of the United States are already waiting to be determined. Iran trembles; Syria, too. And, if all else fails, there is always Cuba or North Korea. The enemy can change in the wink of an eye. The point about arbitrary power is, indeed, that it is arbitrary. What happens once the next lie is told and the next gamble is made? It is perhaps useful to think back to other powerful nations whose leaders liked to lie and loved to gamble—and who won and won and won again until finally they believed their own lies and gambled once too often.

5

States of Despair

History, Politics, and the Struggle for Palestine

Echoes of the Past

Hope is said to have a bitter taste. Nowhere is that more true than in the Middle East, where the possibilities for peace have been squandered and the longings for justice have grown ever more burdensome over the last half century. Worry over the treatment of Arabs by Jews stretches back to the last century over a host of modern Jewish intellectuals, including Hannah Arendt, Martin Buber, Albert Einstein, and Gershom Scholem, among others. But their cautionary warnings were ignored, if not derided, by the Jewish mainstream. It is ironic, since these thinkers implicitly, and sometimes explicitly, anticipated that the Palestinians would shoulder the compensatory costs of the European Holocaust. This historical trick of fate would serve as the source of an ideological competition over who is the *real* victim—a competition that for so long has poisoned the possibility of reasoned debate between Jews and Palestinians.

Jews had, understandably, made a moral demand for a national haven of safety following World War II. Europe, guilt-ridden by its recent past, was willing to sanction one so long as it was somewhere else, such as in the Holy Land. Just as legitimately, however, its Arab inhabitants insisted that they had played no part in the Holocaust and should not be forced to pay such a terrible price for the blood spilled by others. There was one way for Israelis to square the moral circle: understand the creation of the new "Jewish" state as being the provision of "a land without a people for a people without a land." This slogan coined in 1901 by Israel Zangwill, who ironically never believed that it applied to Palestine in the first place, became perhaps *the* founding myth of Israel. It projected the creation of life in an empty desert by a "chosen people," a cultivated people wronged by history who were at last able to build their destiny through intelligence, bravery, and perseverance. Unfortunately, however, the land was not empty or bereft of civilization: it had to be made so.

Herein lies the contribution of the various "revisionist" historians such as Benny Morris and Ilan Pappe, as well as independent-minded sociologists such as Baruch Kimmerling. Their political opinions differ radically, but their research illustrates with scholarly objectivity that the "people without a land" actually created "the land without a people" through what today would be termed "ethnic cleansing." Creating Israel involved forcibly expelling more than 750,000 Arab inhabitants, eliminating more than 400 villages, employing rape and torture, and turning those Arabs living in the new state into second-class citizens to ensure its Jewish character. But the old myth refuses to die. The image still exists of a heroic battle waged by a small community of peaceful Jews against a vast army of savage Arabs, the assault on the Israeli David by the anti-Semitic Goliath, which led to the establishment of the Israeli state in 1948.

War followed war. An attempted seizure of the Suez Canal by Israel with the backing of France and England took place in 1956 until, fearful of increased European influence in the Middle East, the United States demanded that the invaders withdraw. And they did. Then, in 1967, Israel attacked an allied force of Arab armies—from Egypt, Syria, and Jordan—

massing on its borders. The Six-Day War culminated in a humiliating defeat for the Arab world and the capture of the Gaza Strip, the Golan Heights, the Sinai, and the West Bank. It was in response to these events that the Security Council of the United Nations passed the famous Resolution 242, which demanded Israeli withdrawal from the conquered territories. Here began the shift in American policy: Israel now appeared to be the dominant force in the region and a bulkhead against the Soviet Union, with whose interests the Arab world became identified in the eyes of the United States. The National Front for the Liberation of Palestine (Fatah), which was formed in 1959, took over the Palestine Liberation Organization (PLO) when, in 1969, Yasir Arafat was elected its chairman just after it came into existence. Incarnating the demand for a Palestinian state, the PLO was born under the long shadow of the "catastrophe" *(nakba)* of 1948—the expulsion resulting from the creation of Israel—and the disastrous military defeat of 1967.

Cycles of Violence

Terror and denial expressed the desperate reality of defeat and colonial oppression. There followed the hijacking of airplanes, the assassination of eleven Israeli athletes in 1972 at the Munich Olympics, and the PLO's refusal to accept the existence of Israel. The opprobrium heaped on the Arab world and the PLO intensified in 1973 following the surprise attack by Egypt and Syria on Yom Kippur, the holiest day in the Jewish calendar. This culminated in yet another defeat of the Arabs by the Israelis. The money began pouring in from the United States and the Jewish diaspora. A nation under siege faced a nest of terrorists with whom negotiation was impossible. It didn't matter that by 1980 recognizing Israel was on the table or that in 1987, following the Israeli incursion into Lebanon, an intifada spontaneously took shape in Palestine that placed primary emphasis on civil disobedience, a refusal to cooperate with Israeli authorities, and the emergence of a network of nongovernmental organizations to build communal solidarity and resistance. But the imbalance of economic, political, and military power grew in favor of Israel. Settlements were expanded, constrictions on Arabs increased, repression intensified.

By the time the second intifada began in September 2000, Palestinians were facing an Israeli nation that had become the seventh largest military machine in the world, a major arms dealer to previously colonized countries, and the beneficiary of $4 billion per year in foreign aid from the United States. Fifteen thousand people were arrested or sent into exile, had their houses destroyed, or were hurt or killed during and after the first intifada. Committed activists were replaced by inexperienced youths, armed gangs arose, the lure of fundamentalism grew, Palestinian civil society was virtually destroyed, and conditions in the community degenerated. Nearly 3,000 more Palestinians have been killed since September 2000, and more than 300 extrajudicial executions have taken place. That was the context for the new reliance on suicide bombings and organized violence generated during the second intifada, which a militant Palestinian friend told me "did not deserve the name of an *intifada*," and made it different from the earlier uprising.

This most recent action was provoked by Ariel Sharon, who, surrounded by 10,000 troops, walked up the Temple Mount—known to Arabs as *Hareem al-Shareef*, or "noble sanctuary"—as a publicity stunt. A hero to the right-wing religious settlers of the West Bank, Sharon is still despised by the Palestinians for his role in the slaughter of refugees in the Lebanese towns of Shabron and Shitilla in 1982. Sharon's actions at Temple Mount symbolized that Israel still exerts sovereignty not merely over one of the holiest Islamic shrines but over Jerusalem itself. Rioting took place in response to this provocation. The Palestinians attacked with stones, Molotov cocktails, and a few automatic weapons while the Israelis retaliated with live ammunition, antitank rockets, helicopters, and missiles. The Israeli military systematically destroyed the houses of terrorist "sympathizers" and family members; thousands were arrested or tortured; citizens of the occupied territories were denied the most elementary medical and social services; and, finally, construction was begun on more than 750 roadblocks and a huge "wall of separation," for "security" purposes. Jenin was reduced to rubble; nearly half of the 35,000 inhabitants of Hebron left the city, and Qualquilya was closed off from the world for twenty-two days. Since the beginning of the second intifada, more than 2,600 Palestinians, mostly young people, have lost their lives, and more than 24,000 have been wounded, compared with roughly 800 dead and 6,000 wounded among Israelis.

Israel used the eruption of the second intifada to *again* expand the number of Jewish settlements in the occupied territories, further curtail civil liberties, seize Palestinian bank accounts, build a wall, and ward off what Benjamin Netanyahu called "the demographic threat." All this was undertaken by Israel in the name of "security." Elements of the Palestinian resistance, such as Hamas and Hezbollah, then seized upon the idea of suicide bombing. This decision resulted in a moral and political disaster for the Palestinians. Any possibility of capturing the moral high ground was lost. Innocent lives have been destroyed, and the dramatic pictures of the terrorist attacks—young Israelis torn limb from limb in a bombed-out discotheque—tend to overshadow the real if less dramatic oppression that Palestinians suffer every day. A culture of violence was fostered by the new spate of suicide bombings that will undoubtedly leave its mark on the postindependence society.

Hamas has roots in the Palestinian community, since its members provide a host of social services, but other paramilitary groups are little more than gangs of armed thugs that also fight amongst themselves. Sectarian organizations such as these would suffer from *any* peace or the erection of *any* democratic state, and they are placing their own narrow interests over those of the Palestinian people. Their tactics have brought increased repression by the imperialist enemy, and perhaps even worse, they have provided a plausible justification for such repression.

Terror has blocked progress in resolving the crisis, and Edward Said was surely correct in stating the need for a "Palestinian Mandela." Terror has been the ally, not the opponent, of the Israeli occupation. Not to speak out against terrorist tactics and suicide bombings because of some misplaced sense of "solidarity" with the Palestinian people is both self-defeating and an abdication of political responsibility. Such criticism is legitimate, however, only if the systematic institutional exercise of violence by Israel on the Palestinians as a whole is taken into account. Simply indulging in moral outrage over suicide bombings smacks of hypocrisy, especially when Jewish organizations such as the Irgun and the "Stern Gang"—whose leaders Yitzhak Shamir and Menachem Begin later became prime ministers—also employed terrorist tactics in the struggle for independence. A sense of reciprocity, a mixture of political sobriety and moral sensitivity, is required to deal with the conflict between Israelis and Palestinians. Apologies need to be formulated, some sort of compensation must be provided for crimes committed, and "truth and reconciliation" commissions should be assembled to begin the process of psychological healing.

But there is no substitute for a "political" resolution to the conflict. A negotiated settlement—not merely a unilateral withdrawal by Israel—is necessary, if only because the actual territorial claims of both the Jews and the Palestinians still retain a certain arbitrary character. Israel is the product of exiles from a host of other countries who found themselves together in what can only be considered an arbitrarily chosen homeland; Palestine, first institutionally organized by British colonizers who brought the European state model to the Middle East, can justify its borders through little more than historical exigency and a set of resolutions voted on by the United Nations. The arbitrary character of *any* particular territorial solution to the problem has only intensified the appeal of blind nationalism and its ability to be manipulated by elites—especially those who benefit from the existing imbalance of power. Thus, if only for this reason, it is not a matter of proposing one fixed solution or another but rather of articulating flexible demands around which resistance can be mobilized.

The Path from Geneva

Only one serious proposal for peace is on the table, the Geneva Initiative. It was ultimately signed by twenty Israelis and twenty Palestinians, representing a broad spectrum of civil society in the two camps, after more than a year of negotiation. The document lacks any official status, and it is formally recognized by neither Israel nor the Palestinian Authority. But this "treaty," or initiative for peace, has created an enormous controversy among those committed to justice for the Palestinians. It can be seen as the heir of the Oslo talks of 1993 between Yasir Arafat and Yitzhak Rabin or the Camp David talks of 2000 sponsored by President Bill Clinton, though it is predicated on a different approach from the "road map" proposed by President George W. Bush and the quartet of great powers: France, Germany, Great Britain, and Russia. It will surely inform the new or, better, resumed negotiations between Mahmoud Abbas, who was elected leader of the Palestinian Authority following Arafat's death in 2004, and Ariel Sharon. Nevertheless, viewing the new initiative as a dull imitation of the past would be a mistake.

The Geneva Initiative provides a detailed model of a two-state solution to the current conflict, a precise map for the permanent agreement. The framers explicitly chose to move from the large issues to the smaller ones, in contrast to the logic of the "road map." There is also a sense in which each party to the conflict acknowledges the rights of the other—meaning that neither state should infringe on the rights of any of its citizens and, in contrast to previous agreements, that each should exist as a contiguous state. Security would be predicated on turning Palestine into a demilitarized state and subjecting the Israeli military presence to a multinational force. Israel would withdraw to the 1967 border, surrender parts of the Negev adjacent to its border with the Gaza Strip, and keep control of the Wailing Wall. Palestine, for its part, would take control of East Jerusalem and the Temple Mount. The Holy City would be divided in two, and the Old City would become an "open" city. Any negotiated solution will undoubtedly use the Geneva Initiative as its framework.

A two-state solution amenable to Palestinians and Jews has roots in the Balfour Declaration of 1917, which promised Jews a homeland without disrupting any existing Arab communities, and the British white paper of 1922, which divided Palestine into two administrative districts. The two-state solution was explicitly proposed in November 1947 when the General Assembly of the United Nations voted to partition the existing state of Palestine. The Jews accepted, but the Arab leadership, which lacked both foresight and unity, rejected any deal. The offer of 1947 was probably the best one the Palestinians ever received, precisely because Israel was still a dream rather than a superpower. In subsequent years, Israel grew more powerful, and as that occurred, its offers grew more meager while the concessions it demanded from the Palestinian side grew more stark. At the 2000 talks at Camp David, in fact, what remained on the table was only a truncated noncontiguous state in which control over roads, water, and electricity—and of course, security—would remain in the hands of the Israelis. Some felt that the deal was a starting point and should be accepted; others felt that it didn't go far enough and that, essentially, it was a sellout. These arguments are not very different from those surrounding the Geneva Initiative.

But history is a harsh teacher. A comparison of the maps of the two-state solution then and the two-state solution now shows that the longed-for state of Palestine has diminished in both size and the potential for sovereignty. Even if the proposed unilateral withdrawal from Gaza by Israel actually takes place, the result will probably be a Palestinian state essentially composed of various cantons, or Bantustans, rather than a contiguous territory. That is less a product of circumstance than of geopolitical developments that have produced such an extraordinary imbalance of power between the two sides in the struggle. Perhaps it will ultimately prove possible to link the withdrawal from Gaza with a withdrawal from the West Bank. The constraints of the past, however, will probably make themselves felt in future negotiations as well. The terms of any deal will reflect the imbalance of power existing between the two adversaries, and that imbalance is increasingly tilting in favor of Israel.

Urgency speaks in favor of those committed to the Geneva Initiative. Israel is expanding its settlements on the West Bank

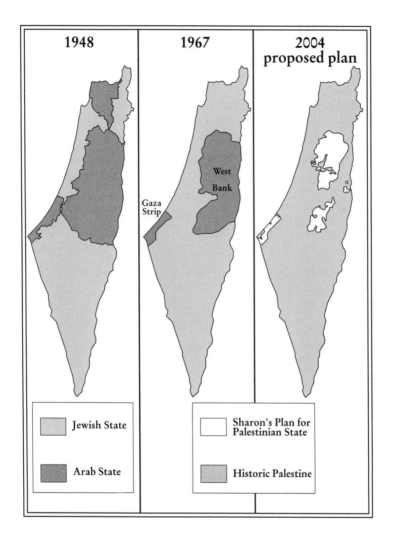

even as its withdrawal from Gaza is being prepared. Mahmoud Abbas has shown a new willingness to crack down on groups that support suicide bombings. New negotiations began in 2005, and it seems that both sides are aware of the catastrophic possibilities if they do not act. Many left-wing critics of the Geneva Initiative, however, believe that the Palestinians have been burned once too often. They maintain that any negotiated two-state solution will inevitably favor Israel and that the only genuine possibility of justice for the Palestinians lies in a binational state. They see Palestinians and Israelis as inextricably bound together by the infrastructure that has been created over the years. To deny this, in their opinion, is to deny reality. Every past attempt at a negotiated peace has, in their view, produced what Tocqueville termed "a crisis of rising expectations," resulting only in increased frustration, mistrust, and a new cycle of violence. Neither the sense of urgency created by the increasingly terrible plight of the Palestinians, nor the new situation generated by Arafat's death, nor the fact that the Geneva Initiative is the only game in town should, in their view, blind citizens to the huge obstacles involved in implementing a two-state solution.

Obstacles and Alternatives

What should be the contours of Palestine? The ideal situation would be for Israel to withdraw to the "green line" or the pre-1967 borders. It would surrender 22 percent of what was left for the Palestinians in 1948 and then annexed in 1967. But first there is the issue of negotiating land that, from the standpoint of the Palestinians, was theirs to begin with. The occupied territories have already been repopulated with more than 200,000 settlers and 160 settlements; of these, according to the Geneva Initiative, 110,000 settlers and 140 settlements would be relocated. But these figures don't include another 200,000 settlers living in parts of the West Bank that were annexed as Jerusalem. Population transfers of this sort are difficult under the best of circumstances, and in this instance, the possibility of violence—and perhaps even civil war—must be taken seriously, given that many inhabitants are ultra-Zionists and religious fanatics. Moreover, these settlements are growing at a rapid pace: 6,000 new Jewish homes are already being planned in the West Bank for 2005. It is not simply that new ones are being built, a matter about which the Israeli government constantly equivocates in public; in addition, the existing settlements are expanding over more and more territory.

Then, too, there is the infrastructure. Land has been seized, water has been placed under control, segregated roads connecting Jewish settlements and disconnecting Palestinian towns have been constructed, and a system of permits and checkpoints has been introduced to immobilize Palestinian citizens. Above all, however, there is the "wall of separation." Still unfinished, 150 kilometers have already been built at a cost of $2.5 million per kilometer. Cutting through the West Bank, the wall rigidly divides towns such as Abu Dis and completely encircles others such as Qualquilya. The wall protects Jewish settlements by creating isolated cantons, ghettos, or Bantustans within the occupied territories that would presumably make up the sovereign state of Palestine. Constructing the wall has enabled Israel to annex fertile Arab lands, destroy arable soil in what remains of the occupied territories, and uproot more than 200,000 trees and olive groves owned by Palestinians. The wall is ruining Arab farmers, hindering Arab workers, and systematically strangling the economies of Arab towns. It has, according to the International Red Cross, enabled Israel to go "far beyond what is permissible for an occupying power under international humanitarian law."

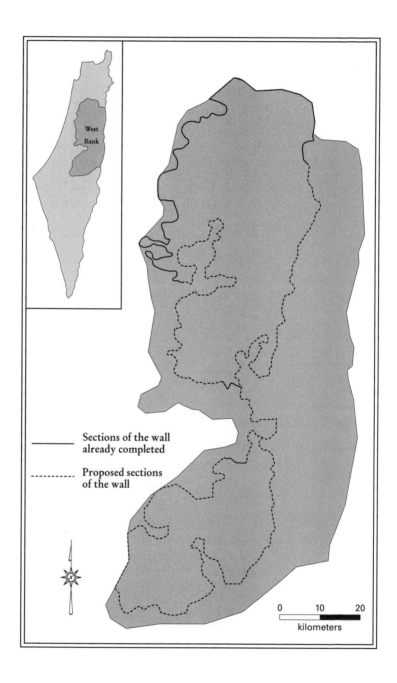

West
Bank

Sections of the wall
already completed

Proposed sections
of the wall

0   10   20
kilometers

But the Geneva Initiative says nothing about any of this. It remains content to note the need for an unspecified "physical barrier" to preserve the security of Israel, even though the wall undermines the prospect of a contiguous and sovereign Palestine. Critics of the Geneva Initiative suggest that only an overriding effort from within a binational state has the possibility of bringing down the wall. It is the same when dealing with the "right of return." Atrocities committed throughout history are seen by Israel as legitimating a right of return for all Jews. But the Geneva Initiative expects a waiver of this right by descendants of the dispossessed inhabitants of Palestine, who now number roughly 3.5 million people living in refugee camps under unspeakable conditions. The return of Palestinians to Israel would, after all, change the demographic composition of the Jewish state and compromise the right of return for those Jews confronted with anti-Semitism in the future.

Advocates of the Geneva Initiative essentially claim that allowing for the right of return would torpedo any peace agreement. Israelis will not accept abandonment of a Jewish state, and most Palestinians, it is argued, would prefer their own state rather than the unrealizable dream of a binational state. But it is also unlikely that 3.5 million Palestinians would exercise the right of return, and monetary compensation, similar to what the German Jews received from the postwar German government, might be offered as an alternative. Without some explicit policy, however, the right of return will weigh on every attempt at reconciliation. Marketing any version of the Geneva Initiative will prove difficult if it appears that peace is being exchanged for justice or if the unilateral withdrawal from Gaza, without reference to the West Bank, comes to define the "moderate" response to right-wing fanaticism.

Other obstacles to a two-state solution deserve consideration. The assumption made by those who framed the Geneva

Initiative is that two genuine democracies will emerge from an officially signed treaty. But this claim invites skepticism. Within Israel, even without considering the occupied territories, Arabs already constitute more than 20 percent of the population, and what is now generally termed an internal "demographic threat" is growing. Excluded from the political mainstream in a variety of ways, Israeli Arabs have been the victims of discrimination and a radically unequal distribution of services. Integrating them into society and providing them with equality will increasingly threaten the Jewish character of the state. It is not difficult to see a growing tension between the mutually exclusive demands of preserving the Jewish identity of Israel and maintaining its democratic commitments.

As for Palestine, it lacks liberal political traditions, a bureaucratic infrastructure, an indigenous bourgeoisie, and, possibly, a sovereign authority capable of securing what Max Weber considered decisive: a monopoly over the means of coercion. Palestine, too, will face the conflict between satisfying its orthodox religious groups and building a secular republic. It will also have to deal with elements of the population that are unwilling to recognize the "second state" (Israel). Not simply a Palestinian state but a democratic state with an accountable bureaucracy and a centralized security apparatus will need the legitimacy and power required to crack down on the various organized groups of religious fanatics and secular thugs whose interests oppose a negotiated peace. The situation is only made more difficult by the fact that so many thousands of settlements will have been built in the West Bank before Gaza has even been evacuated and that Israel has retained the right to intervene whenever it deems necessary, as well as control over water, roads, and other elements of the infrastructure.

The vision of a binational state seemingly solves many of the deficiencies associated with the two-state solution proposed by the Geneva Initiative. Border problems and security arrangements would obviously be settled. The wall of separation would be eliminated, and the privileges currently accorded Jewish citizens and settlers would be abolished, along with attempts to identify the state with either Islam or Judaism. The binational state would also offer an elegant solution to the problem of return by guaranteeing it to both Palestinians and Jews. The new binational state could make use of the bureaucracy and institutional political arrangements that are already in place. Palestinians would have an incentive to embrace liberal democracy, since they would constitute the majority, and it would be in the interest of Israelis to respect civil liberties in order to protect their status as a minority. With a binational state, it might finally be possible to speak about a lasting peace and a state that could come to terms with its neighbors and fit into the overriding culture of the Middle East.

A binational solution, however, presupposes a great deal. It calls for a suspension of mistrust inherited from the past and the abolition of solidarity based on religion and ethnicity. Ignoring the emotional power of "identity" and the role of religious emotions in shaping the current conjuncture, supporters of the binational solution must depend on the willingness of both Israelis and Palestinians to extend their loyalty to a secular state. It is also hard to imagine the smooth integration of an advanced bureaucratic state with the rudimentary structure of a resistance movement that has not yet created a state with a monopoly over the means of coercion. Nor is there much of a fit between the political traditions of Israel and Palestine. Again, proponents of the Geneva Initiative are surely correct in noting that there is no mechanism for translating the vision of a binational state into reality.

Privileging the two-state solution is unavoidable. But it might be useful to consider—for the long term—a third option that combines the best of the two-state solution and the binational state. The historical precedent is, interestingly enough, the English proposals of 1947, which essentially envisioned a *confederation* based on two relatively autonomous political states connected by an economic union, with uniform standards for labor and commerce. Arafat himself, in fact, often proposed a type of Benelux model for the region that would include Israel, Palestine, and Jordan. Under such a scenario, ethnic and religious identifications would remain in place. But political conflict could diminish through the incentives attendant on an economic union. Prospects of investment in Palestine, along with wages and benefits equal to those in Israel, might provide a material foundation for security and the elimination of old territorial ambitions. But there is also little doubt that proponents of such a confederation would have to deal with many of the same obstacles facing supporters of the two-state solution and a binational state—first and foremost, the continuing intransigence of Israel.

Concluding Remarks

Meaningful pressure from the United States to bring about a resolution is unlikely. President Bush is not willing to "ride herd" on the most powerful party to the conflict in the Middle East. He called on the participants in the conflict to begin with small points of agreement and then work up to a Palestinian state, but his plan lacked any enforcement mechanism or serious incentives for Israel to restrain its imperialist appetite. Even if the Republicans were to take a more balanced approach, it is quite possible that the Democrats would uncritically identify themselves with Israeli ambitions; such a tactic could improve their chances in the next election. Neither American political party, it seems, is willing to call for disinvestments or to curb the $4 billion per year in U.S. aid and the $9 million in loans to Israel to help bring about an end to the occupation.

Social movements in the United States and Europe, therefore, have an important role to play in shaping public opinion. First, however, they must distinguish between the legitimate security concerns of the Israeli state and the inflated ideals of Zionism. The old vision is obviously eroding. According to recent polls, 65 percent believe that Israel is crumbling economically, and 73 percent believe that it is crumbling socially. A palpable sense of despair is taking hold that is only intensified by the ever-present danger of terrorist attacks and the growing belief that Israel is turning into a pariah nation. But there is also a sense of denial that has grasped the Israeli mainstream and is difficult for outsiders to understand. Instead of thinking about the impact of Israeli policy on Palestine and the Arab world, instead of considering that Israel's actions might be increasing sympathy for the victims of the occupation, secular Zionists and religious zealots now choose to preoccupy themselves with the emergence of a "new anti-Semitism."

The only thing new about the new anti-Semitism is that the geographic terrain has shifted and Jews are no longer fragmented among themselves or the powerless victims of a Christian world. Jews now have a powerful homeland, powerful lobbying organizations in all the Western democratic states, and powerful allies like the United States. Today, there are no fascist organizations fueled by anti-Semitic ideology; anti-Semitism is not taught in the Western world, and biological racism is unacceptable in polite society; there is no anti-Semitic movement in any of the democracies with any serious possibility of attaining power. A synagogue is defaced, a cemetery is desecrated, a Jewish individual is molested in the street. These are terrible and inexcusable acts. Interpreting them in terms of the 1930s, however, can only produce profound misunderstandings. Any serious American engagement with the politics of the Middle East must begin by rejecting historical analogies of this sort; current Israeli politics cannot be justified by making reference to the Holocaust, and each and every criticism of Israeli policies is not an act of anti-Semitism.

Many Jews are tired of having what is best about their tradition associated with militarism, imperialism, religious obscurantism, and the most blatant racism. More than 60 percent of the Israeli citizenry favors some kind of two-state solution to the current crisis. Various nongovernmental organizations such as Peace Now and groups such as Women in Black, along with the "refuseniks"—soldiers unwilling to serve in the occupied territories—are laying the foundation for a civil society significantly different from the one that currently exists. The activities undertaken by such courageous groups do not deserve the lack of coverage accorded them by the mainstream American media. Publicizing the degree of domestic opposition in Israel can break the prevalent image that all Jews are united behind an imperialist and racist enterprise in the occupied territories. Similarly, there is the stereotypical image of Palestinians as bloodthirsty zealots intent only on driving the Jews into the sea. Those intent on seeking peace must indeed be vigilant in opposing the ambitions of groups within Israel and Palestine that are opposed to peace.

The political landscape has not been transformed by the work of the Far Right in Israel or by the self-defeating violence of Hamas and Hezbollah. Rather, it has been transformed by the proposal for a unilateral withdrawal from Gaza, along with the election of Mahmoud Abbas by the Palestinians. No longer is it possible for fanatics on either side to maintain that there is no viable partner in seeking a negotiated settlement. Understandably, a majority of Israelis and Palestinians would greet the resumption of talks with enthusiasm. Enemies on either side of the divide offer little more than an objective apology for imperialism. Leftists in the United States and Europe should treat their appeals in that spirit.

Creating institutions capable of providing for democratic self-determination by inhabitants of the occupied territories should be the principal aim of those interested in the future of Palestine. Support should be given to doubling the existing aid package to rebuild the infrastructure in the occupied territories—it could reach $6 billion over four years—under the auspices of an international consortium composed of the United States, the European Union, and various Arab states. Combined with new pressure on Israel to ease the burden imposed by internal roadblocks and the wall, such aid would help solidify the foundations for a new regime. But the plan is now to cut American aid from an already meager $200 to $600 million even though the reconstruction of the occupied territories might help bring about an agreement between the two sides to the conflict.

But aid is only a first step. Dealing with the wall is a precondition for *any* viable solution to the conflict. That Israel has legitimate security concerns is undeniable, and if the current wall had been constructed along the pre-1967 borders, there would probably be little debate. As things stand, however, the existing wall has produced an annexation of more lands. Although Israeli security may require a physical barrier, it need not rest on the combination of ditches, barricades, barbed wire, and numerous checkpoints that humiliate the populace daily, devastate the environment, strangle the economy in the occupied territories, and fragment the community. Palestine has already called for condemnation of the wall by the International Court of Justice at the Hague, whose jurisdiction on this matter is denied by both Israel and the United States. The United Nations has overwhelmingly voted in favor of the wall's removal. Israeli civil rights groups have also, with some degree of success, brought the legality of the wall of separation before the Israeli Supreme Court. But even though some kilometers of the wall will now be destroyed in the encircled town of Baka al Sharkyeh, which complements the strategy of unilateral withdrawal, new construction in Beit Seira, Beit Surik, parts of Jerusalem, and elsewhere is continuing at a rapid pace. *The wall must fall,* as the popular slogan demands. Making good on that demand is a precondition for creating a functional Palestinian state, a confederation, or a binational arrangement.

An enduring peace is difficult to imagine without an end to the occupation. This can only mean Israel's withdrawal to the pre-1967 borders and either the abandonment of the Jewish settlements *tout court,* with an eye toward creating a functional Palestinian state, or their integration into a binational solution to the crisis. Leaving settlements within Palestine, especially those that "cantonize" the future nation, will obviously undercut the substantive exercise of sovereignty and also create an irredentist minority within the new state. Conflicting conceptions of the character of compromise, however, cannot be elided if the two sides to the conflict are going to engage directly in the peace process. Israel considers itself the claimant to the lands under discussion; it sees itself as the victor in a flurry of wars, and it perceives its enemy as stubborn and recalcitrant. By the same token, Palestinians maintain that any negotiated peace will be predicated on what they—not the Israelis—are willing to concede, because *all* the land under discussion was taken from the Palestinians in the first place.

Recognizing this reality, if for no other reason, makes it necessary to end the silence over the right of return. The issue can conceivably be resolved in terms of Palestinians being allowed to exercise this right, being provided with monetary compensation for relinquishing it, or being given a choice between the two. Some degree of imagination and flexibility will be necessary in formulating an acceptable package. Under no circumstances, however, can an acceptable peace—a peace with legitimacy—be achieved by sacrificing justice.

Treaties are unnecessary between friends, and compromises are irrelevant when opponents share the same interest. The compromises required for any settlement of the conflict between Israel and Palestine can always be understood as a betrayal of ethnic, national, or religious ambitions. No treaty can compensate for past injustices or sacrifices undertaken in the name of the cause. Any real possibility of dealing with the deeper problems and the more acute feelings of injury requires a new public attitude that shows less concern for passions than for interests. The Bible and the Koran won't help in solving the conflict. The language of national security no less than national self-determination has been corrupted. Public intellectuals in the United States and elsewhere have a role to play in mitigating the sense of hopeless frustration and squashing the hope for a utopian solution. They can indeed help foster the requisite combination of liberalism and realism necessary for suspending the prospect of protracted violence and, ultimately, developing a culture of reconciliation.

6

Anatomy of a Disaster

*Class War, Iraq, and the Contours of
American Foreign Policy*

Lest We Forget

There was a new game in town after President Bush declared: "Mission accomplished!" The political establishment decided it was time to forget the lies and blunders associated with the Iraqi war. Europe was ready to reaffirm its bonds with the United States, the United Nations was trying to placate the superpower, and smaller nations were desperately trying to make a deal. The angry demonstrations of the past, the loss of "the street," no longer seemed relevant. It was time to "get on with the job" of securing the peace. June 30, 2005, has passed, however, and American troops are still in Iraq. American soldiers are dying, bombings in public areas occur daily, and there is no end in sight to the violence. Elections took place in January 2005. The Sunnis boycotted them, the Kurds kept speaking of an independent state, and the voters chose from lists of anonymous candidates. No consensus was achieved, the character of the future constitution is uncertain, and the legitimacy of the new state will assuredly remain weak for a long time to come. Major cities such as Adamiya, Karbala, Kufa, Najaf, Shula, and Falluja—with its 300,000 inhabitants—have been mercilessly bombed, invaded by tanks, and turned into virtual ghost towns. A pattern of prisoner abuse has further undermined the already plummeting image of the United States throughout the region.

Democracy in Iraq is a hope, at best, not a reality. It is the same with the victory proclaimed by President Bush so many months ago. Precisely for that reason, however, it is important to recall how the American public was manipulated, the world bullied, and the fragile nature of the democratic discourse endangered by an administration whose declaration of war was inspired by imperialist fantasies and guided by reactionary ambitions. New crises are already presenting themselves in Iran and Syria, and it seems that the Bush administration is employing the same strategic mixture of deceit and belligerence. Too often ignored, however, is the way that this imperialist foreign policy, fueled by militarism and hypernationalism, is cloaking a new domestic form of class war. Battling the latter calls for understanding the former. This turns the need to remember into a political issue.

Winning the Hearts and Minds

There are countless dictators in the world, and Saddam, bad as he was, was probably not the most gruesome. The United States cannot intervene everywhere. The question is why an intervention should have taken place in Iraq. It has now been revealed that Saddam actually made various last-minute overtures to avoid war; his concessions apparently included unrestricted investigations for nuclear weapons by American inspectors and even free elections. Perhaps the offer was fraudulent. We'll never know. Whatever the possibility for peace or the prospect of negotiations, it was never taken seriously. But that's not all. Reports by the State Department forecast the difficulties associated with rebuilding the Iraqi infrastructure, the looting that would follow the opening of the prisons, and the resentment that would greet American troops. These reports were also ignored.

Two major studies by American experts commissioned by the Bush administration, one by David Kay and the other by Charles Duelfer, state that Saddam Hussein was not building nuclear arms or in the possession of large quantities of chemical weapons; it seems that his nuclear program was abandoned in 1991 and his chemical weapons program in 1996. Meanwhile, Secretary of State Colin Powell admitted long ago that no proof existed of an Iraq–al Qaeda link. This obviously undermines the claim that Iraq constituted a genuine threat, let alone *the* genuine threat, to the national security of the United States. As for the claim that the purpose of the invasion was to further democracy in the region: staunch American allies such as Kuwait and Saudi Arabia, even after a limited experiment with municipal elections, are not exactly testaments to the democratic spirit. Nor can the invasion be considered a logical outcome of the assault on Afghanistan, in which a genuine international coalition supported an attack on the Taliban regime because of its clear complicity in the events of 9/11. Richard Haas, president of the Council on Foreign Relations, put the matter well: "Iraq was a war of choice, not a war that had to be fought."

The American public would never have supported the war against Iraq if it had been given the information available now. Military force was already deemed "inevitable" by July 2002, and human rights became a fashionable justification for the war only after other justifications lost their validity. The pro-war clique of "realists" in the Department of Defense made their reputations, after all, by attacking "idealists" who favored human rights. Current Secretary of Defense Donald Rumsfeld offered support to Saddam in 1984, during the Iran-Iraq War, as a special envoy of the Reagan administration, with full knowledge of the chemical weapons used against the Kurds. Deputy Secretary of Defense Paul Wolfowitz actually stated in *Vanity*

Fair in June 2003 that although freedom from the tyranny of Saddam Hussein was an important aim of American policy in Iraq, this alone was "not a reason to put the lives of American kids at risk."

All the claims have been shot down. Ahmed Chalabi, a prime source for allegations of the existence of weapons of mass destruction, now states, "we are heroes in error." The best the administration can do is declare that Iraq's continuing search for arms justified the war and launch an investigation into the sources of the "false information" fed to the president. Debate over the illusory claims and the quality of information has produced a loss of memory concerning the real reasons for the war: geopolitical dreams of controlling vast oil resources and four rivers—the Greater and Lesser Zab as well as the Tigris and Euphrates—in one of the most arid regions of the world; intimidation of Tehran, Damascus, and the Palestinians; a belief that American interests in the Middle East can no longer be left in the hands of Israel; and the perceived need for an alternative to the military bases situated in the increasingly archaic and potentially explosive nation of Saudi Arabia. Indeed, the United States felt that its presence in the region was required; larger interests than those of Iraq were at stake.

President Bush insisted after 9/11 that the war on terror would last a long time: years, decades, perhaps even generations. There was no single identifiable enemy—only an amorphous transnational terrorist movement and a shifting collection of rogue states harboring fanatics and preparing for nuclear war. The enemy could be anywhere; its hatred could only be irrational. Thus, with a paranoia sparked by the dreadful events of 9/11, and the flames of hysteria fanned by the administration's exaggerations, the Bush administration began to think anew about various calls to reconfigure the Middle East. Paul O'Neill, the former secretary of the treasury, stated openly that President Bush and his top aides had begun talking of eliminating Saddam in the earliest days of the administration. Leading architects of the war, such as Wolfowitz and Perle, had argued for the ouster of Saddam as early as 1991, and it made sense for the Bush administration to take seriously the contingency plans formulated in September 2000 by neoconservative think tanks such as Project for the New American Century. These reports insisted on the strategic importance of dominating the Gulf as well as creating a "worldwide command and control system" to deal with nations such as North Korea, Iran, and Syria, which President Bush would later lump together and condemn as the "axis of evil."

Fighting the Good Fight

The "war on terror," if that phrase still has any meaning, is not going away. Right-wing politicians in Washington continue to joke: "Sissies stay in Baghdad; real men want Tehran and Damascus." Every now and then, a trial balloon goes up expressing new fears about this or that "rogue" state. It is lambasted for aiding the attacks on American troops, harboring or selling nuclear weapons, and imperiling the stability of the Middle East and the world. By the same token, however, public skepticism for yet another military adventure has grown. American forces are now stretched thin. The economic and military miscalculations made in Iraq have put the Bush administration on the defensive. Its foreign policy is in shambles. Nevertheless, that can change.

Relations between Europe and the United States will undoubtedly improve; an ongoing confrontation would make no sense. Both are too politically important, too economically powerful, and too alike. The rifts remaining within the European Union require mending, which is possible only through a rapprochement with the United States, and the hegemon ultimately needs reliable allies. The United Nations, for its part, has now passed a resolution supporting American policy in Iraq. That, too, only makes sense. The UN cannot remain at loggerheads with its most powerful member; such a course would spell financial disaster and instability for the organization. Some degree of international cooperation concerning the future of Iraq is inevitable, but tensions remain. Symbolic support is different from military support, and although it is apparent that the United States cannot bear the costs of reconstructing the country by itself, the billions in aid sought by the Bush administration are not forthcoming.

But it is not simply a matter of money. The "coalition of the willing," composed of the bribed and the bullied, is disintegrating: Spain, Poland, and Hungary have withdrawn their troops, while Bulgarian, Dominican, Honduran, Nicaraguan, and South Korean support has been drastically scaled back. The Bush administration is no longer concerned with the moral high ground accorded the United States following the tragedy of 9/11. It knows that the peoples of most nations now see the United States as the primary threat to world peace and as a hypocrite willing to make war on weak states and then leave the mess to be cleaned up by others. Even in Latin America, in a poll taken during the first week of January 2004, Zogby International found that 87 percent of "opinion makers" in the region disapproved of Bush's foreign policy; another poll found that nearly a third of all Latin Americans, a twofold increase since 2000, had a negative image of the United States. The world senses that the constructive criticism of democratic allies is no longer taken seriously. The Bush administration has been advised by its own panel of experts that "hostility toward America has reached shocking levels" among Muslims and that the "image" of the United States must change.

The source of a new public-relations campaign, however, will surely not be Afghanistan. Elections have taken place in part of the country, but 40 percent of the population is living below the subsistence level, and the prospect of starvation haunts more than 6 million inhabitants (*New York Times,* December 12, 2004). Afghanistan is also witnessing a revival of the Taliban amid the armed conflicts between tribal chieftains and drug lords, similar to the battles between American gangsters during Prohibition, and there is precious little sense of a deep commitment to reconstruction. The stable, secular, and democratic regime promised by the Bush administration has not materialized. Admittedly, some financial and humanitarian aid has been given to Afghanistan by the allies of the United States in its internationally supported military response to the Taliban regime harboring the criminals of 9/11. President Bush has offered a measly $15 million, and further aid is assuredly imperiled by demands for support in Iraq. This is not a good sign. Afghanistan is now ranked 173 out of 178 countries by the United Nations' 2004 Human Development Index. Any potential ally would get the impression that American foreign policy is at cross-purposes in that part of the world. It is.

There is nothing worse than a fearful bully; feint and retreat, destroy and leave, have supplanted any sustained foreign policy or commitment to reconstruction. Buffeted between bellicose rhetoric and uncertain aims, the Bush administration is adrift. Some half-cracked officials and advisers of this administration think that the cure, the best way to soften the impact of a failed policy in Iraq, is to gamble on a spectacular victory elsewhere. Joining control of Iran with that exercised by the United States over Afghanistan and Iraq is surely a tempting possibility for the architects of the war, and the imperialist fantasies of the lunatic Right should not be underestimated. A submissive Syria—now accused of interference in Iraqi affairs and support of terrorists—might offer a corrective. But Iran is the greater prize precisely because, ironically, the tumbling of Saddam has left it as the dominant Islamic power in the region. So in January 2005, the United States began flying planes over Syria and conducting secret reconnaissance missions inside Iran to locate potential nuclear, chemical, and missile sites. It may all lead to nothing, but it's better to follow Machiavelli and Sun Tzu and prepare for the worst.

The Price of Victory

The cost of the Iraqi war has been far higher than anyone expected, and it will not be paid for a long time. More is involved than dollars and cents. American democracy has incurred dramatic wounds. The Left laughs at those who would substitute the term *liberty fries* for *french fries,* but it is no laughing matter. A wave of nationalism and xenophobia has been unleashed in a country that clearly retains what the great American historian Richard Hofstadter called a "paranoid streak." Coupled with the introduction of legislation like the Patriot Act, there have been calls by the Right for an "academic bill of rights" and threats to lift funding from institutes that are too critical of Israel and American foreign policy. Neoconservatives are expanding federal death penalty statutes and issuing subpoenas without the approval of judges or grand juries, insisting on maximum penalties while limiting plea bargaining, and constricting the right to counsel, bail, habeas corpus, and freedom from surveillance. A "watch list" of more than 100,000 suspects associated with terrorism is currently being designed. Justification for such measures is supplied by a seemingly endless number of "national security alerts" for which neither criteria nor evidence is ever supplied.

Congress, admittedly, set up two "bipartisan" committees to "investigate" the administration. In concert with a cowed and simpering media, however, they have tended to sweep under the carpet the sheer incompetence of and blatant misuse of power by the Bush administration. Every now and then a little gem is still dropped. For example, the public learns about the formation of a company known as New Bridge Strategies, composed of businessmen close to the family and administration of President Bush, which is consulting other companies seeking slices of taxpayer-financed reconstruction projects.

The mainstream media lost their bearings amid the outburst of euphoric nationalism that accompanied the outbreak of hostilities. But whether this ongoing laxity is due to intellectual laziness, a "club" mentality, or misplaced pragmatism is irrelevant. Independent-minded people now look to other sources of information, such as the Internet. There they can find writings by a host of critics who insisted from the beginning that Iraq had no serious links to al Qaeda, that it constituted no threat to the security of the United States, and that Iraqi oil revenues would not pay for a "short" war. There they can find commentators who anticipated that the people of Iraq would not embrace the United States as a liberator and that any number of serious, if not intractable, problems would plague the postwar reconstruction.

Two hundred billion dollars have already been spent on the Iraqi conflict in two years. Even before adding on other budget requests totaling between $70 billion and $100 billion, the huge surplus inherited from the Clinton administration has turned into the largest deficit in the history of the United States. Tax cuts that benefit the rich exacerbate the situation, profits are not reinvested, and low-paying jobs without benefits are being substituted for high-paying jobs with benefits. The richest 1 percent of Americans acquired more after-tax money than the bottom 40 percent combined, yet the nation remains in an economic downturn, thereby rendering new social programs unfeasible. Although wars have traditionally been associated with an expansion of domestic programs—consider the GI Bill in the aftermath of World War II or the complex of social programs associated with the Great Society during the conflict in Vietnam—that has not been the case this time.

Soldiers will have it much tougher when they return. Work requirements have been increased for welfare recipients, overtime has been eliminated for more than two million workers, child-care subsidies have been reduced throughout the country, and there is barely a single welfare program that has not felt the knife; a particularly mean-spirited example is the virtual elimination of a tiny program costing $150 million to tutor the children of convicts. The union rights of workers employed in the many agencies connected with the Office of Homeland Security have also been rolled back. Then there are the lives wasted and, especially for the Iraqis, the "collateral damage." The price of this conflict was purposely underestimated, later miscalculated, and now understated by the current administration. If ever there were a president who deserved to be impeached, it is George W. Bush.

False Hope

There will be no quick transition to democracy in Iraq. Its citizens have not welcomed their liberators, terror remains rampant, and the obstacles to reconstruction are enormous. We still have the prospect of a protracted war and a long occupation. How long? Some in the administration argue that America should cut its losses; others, such as former director of the National Security Council and current secretary of state Condoleezza Rice, insist that Americans might have to remain in Iraq for a generation. In order to justify his policy, the president has claimed that Iraq is now the "central front" in the international war against terror. Is that because terrorists are flowing into the country from Iran and Syria? Or has there been a profound misunderstanding of the national resistance against the American invasion? With respect to Iraq, it hardly makes sense to speak of terror any longer; it's better to think of the situation as a traditional guerrilla war against an imperialist military occupier and its collaborators.

Knee-jerk responses won't help matters; the situation is complex. Although most Baghdadis look forward to the creation of a democratic order and probably believe that life will improve for them in five years, different groups within Iraqi society have very different notions of what democracy means and what institutions should govern the new polity. The constitutional efforts by the provisional government must deal with profound disagreements over whether this new regime should take the form of a Western parliamentary democracy or an Islamic republic. Rifts also run deep between Sunni and Shiite Muslims, between moderates and fundamentalists within the Shiite community itself, and between various minorities on the borders of Iraq. Not merely the degree of nationalism in Iraq but also the depth of competing ethnoreligious identification are intense. It remains unclear which is more powerful.

Maintaining or increasing American troop levels will most likely plunge Iraq into deeper chaos and ultimately empower a new set of antidemocratic forces. Creating an Iraqi military and police force sounds good, but terror directed against the population and the regime is undermining the effort. Leaders of the 50,000 Iraqis already recruited are coming from the old regime. Tribal chieftains, gangsters, and the new leaders of paramilitary organizations will also not simply disappear. In contrast to the Bush administration's initial claims that opposition is strong only among "dead-enders," such as foreign religious fanatics and criminal gangs, according to most assessments, everyday Iraqis are becoming increasingly disgusted with the U.S. military occupation, and among much of the population, collaborators are treated like traitors. Introducing substitute forces from the United Nations or Europe might provide a solution, but that will not happen as long as command remains a prerogative of the United States. Senator Edward Kennedy has already stated publicly that Iraq is turning into "President Bush's Vietnam." The same logic is in effect: It cannot be that the entire undertaking is a failure. If only more troops were sent, then. . . . Of course, there is a way out of Iraq—just as there was a way out of Vietnam. It is a matter of setting a timetable for withdrawal while negotiating with other nations in the region and the United Nations to train Iraqi militia and police. That is only one option. So far, however, no exit strategy has been *politically* acceptable to the Bush administration and its mainstream critics.

Support should be given to the new democratic institutions. But their legitimacy is questionable given the economic devastation, the lack of a functioning bureaucracy, and the authoritarian legacy whose scars the Iraqi citizens still bear. The contradiction is clear: the new Iraqi regime must prove itself but the United States must remain to prop it up. The ideological reason is most likely the general strategic decision to reject the multilateral foreign policy of the past—with its reliance on NATO, the UN, and various regional associations of states—in favor of a unilateral approach. But there are also practical reasons. Domestic politics cannot simply be divorced from foreign policy. The provincial mass base of political support for the Bush administration has never had any use for the

United Nations, and it has always understood NATO to be an arm for implementing American foreign policy goals. Conservative elites are adamant that American corporations closely tied to the administration retain their lucrative contacts for reconstructing Iraq and its oil industry, while the Christian coalition and other groups imbued with nationalistic ideology expect the retention of its new military basis. These reactionary groups would be furious if an "apology" for the invasion were made or the "victory" compromised.

When the Iraqi war broke out, without any sense of the different power constellations, references were constantly made to the consequences of appeasing Hitler in the 1930s. Next the postwar era was invoked. Iran and Syria and other Middle Eastern states have been challenged by the United States to embrace democratic "regime change," just as Europe did following the defeat of Nazism. That is a laudable goal. But it becomes little more than posturing for domestic consumption, or a veiled threat to the axis of evil, when democracy is upheld by tanks and coupled with direct imperialist exploitation. The Middle East lacks the indigenous traditions of liberalism and social democracy that marked European history. The context is radically different, and the analogy is false.

Authoritarian populism is the most likely outcome in Iraq: a strong president in an illiberal regime with democratic ornaments. It might be useful to think about what might be termed neofascism, or *Saddam light*. The existential no less than the economic plight of the population makes such an outcome likely. In the aftermath of World War I, a defeated Germany was forced to admit sole responsibility for the conflict, compensate the victorious allies, and surrender part of its territory, while its new democratic leaders were castigated as "November criminals" and "traitors" for supposedly collaborating with the enemy and signing the Treaty of Versailles. Nationalist fervor arose among the masses and among the soldiers; the latter, who were largely unemployed following the peace, formed any number of right-wing paramilitary organizations. Chaos followed the war, left-wing revolutions were attempted, the economy collapsed, unemployment raged, and liberal politicians were assassinated at a rapid rate. The new republic never gained the legitimacy its framers expected, and dreams of revenge festered.

Iraq in 2003 is obviously not Germany in 1918. But even though there have been no left-wing revolutionary uprisings in postwar Iraq, unemployment is now about 70 percent, and similar preconditions for a new form of fascism are striking. A defeated nation—billions in debt to a variety of countries— must take responsibility for a war that was obviously the work of its enemy; this same enemy has instituted economic policies intent on privatizing 200 Iraqi firms, allowing 100 percent ownership of Iraqi industries and banks by foreign investors, and making it legal for all profits to be sent abroad. The new leaders of Iraq fear for their lives. Other than religious figures such as the Grand Ayatollah Ali el Sistani, whose preference is for a state under some form of Islamic law, they inspire little enthusiasm and less trust. It would seem that any new Western-styled regime will suffer from a deficit of legitimacy. Iraq has been humiliated, its infrastructure destroyed, and its national fabric frayed.

So far, Republican policy makers have not felt chastened by the catastrophe they unleashed. President Bush has said publicly that God told him to invade Iraq. And with a new group of ideologically driven senators, more militaristic exploits loom ahead, especially if there is another terror attack on American soil. Saber rattling is already taking place over nuclear buildups in North Korea and Iran. Syria is constantly being castigated for its support of terrorists and even for hiding weapons of mass destruction. New military incursions into other nations might take place just to paper over a failed policy in Iraq. The battle of Falluja has caused the destruction of nearly half the 120 mosques in the city. Two-thirds of the 300,000 citizens living in Falluja have been forced to abandon their homes, and the death toll is high. American troops entered an empty city, because whoever the real terrorists might have been, they escaped, drew back, and began to regroup while enemy factions among them were forging a new unity.

More cities and neighborhoods are surely going to be obliterated. Creating democracy will not be easy with the infrastructure destroyed, unemployment skyrocketing, a still illegitimate government, a lack of basic security, and the Sunnis feeling like outcasts. More than 100,000 Iraqis and 1,500 Americans have already died in a war whose original justification was blatant mendacity and demagoguery; this sullies the term *democracy,* in whose name it is supposedly being fought.

The president intends to send more troops into Iraq while seeking to make its new government self-sufficient and independent. But how that will be accomplished remains unclear. The United States is intent on keeping its military bases, its reconstruction contracts, and, obviously, a regime loyal to its wishes. Pursuing such aims will surely fuel nationalist sentiments, recruit more supporters for terrorist groups in the region, and keep America deeply enmeshed in Iraqi affairs well into the future. The president himself said, in an honest moment, that the war on terror can't be won. That is also the case for an Iraqi war waged without concern for international law or the feelings of traditional allies, without a genuine mass base of support inside the country, and without an exit strategy.

Neither a civil war, which might destabilize the region even more, nor a partition, which would generate a permanent irredentism among Iraqis, is a far-fetched possibility. Nationalism provides the only locus of unity, which translates into hatred of the invader. Resistance to the United States is rapidly becoming a symbol for the anti-Western and antidemocratic fundamentalists in the region; linkage between Iraqi insurgents and "terrorist" forces, precisely what the Bush administration most feared, is actually coming to pass. America has responded to this situation by employing police and military officers of the old regime while making deals with tribal chieftains and religious leaders. These are not reliable allies; neither by tradition nor by inclination are they disposed to democracy, and it is becoming easier to imagine the emergence of a new authoritarian state lacking in gratitude to its creators and politically incapable of guaranteeing the United States a presence in the region. Perhaps things will turn out differently. But the future does not look bright for the forces of liberty.

A Class War

When the twentieth century began, among the Left in the socialist labor movement, it was generally believed that imperialism, militarism, and nationalism were the natural fruits of an inevitably more exploitative capitalism. That perspective is no longer fashionable. Even now, *imperialism* is a word rarely used in polite company, and talking about a "system" is considered old-fashioned. History is interpreted by many on the Left as an agglomeration of ruptures and contingencies. To be sure, speaking about inevitability is misleading, and there is little left of orthodox Marxism. But still, imperialism, militarism, and heightened nationalism are functioning together today amid an intense economic assault on working people and the poor. Not to see the interconnection among these phenomena undermines the ability to make sense of world affairs and respond to what more than one Nobel Prize winner has called the most reactionary administration in American history.

Imperialism need not benefit the nation as a whole nor be purely economic in character. It can serve only certain small, powerful interests, and it can project primarily geopolitical aims. But the profits can be enormous—Halliburton has already recorded contracts worth $9.6 billion, and another $6 billion per year is projected—and increased control over resources such as water and oil will have a regional impact. There is nothing strange in suggesting that the reconstruction contracts awarded to certain American firms and the economic arrangements introduced into Iraq, coupled with geopolitical control of regional resources, are part of a new imperialist strategy undertaken by the United States, the *hegemon,* in a period marked by globalization. It cannot be a coincidence that rogue states almost always are traditional in orientation, exist outside the orbit of global society, and have a citizenry that is brown or black. The United States is already harshly criticizing Iran and Syria for failing to close borders, for building nuclear arms, and for posing a threat to planetary security. The propaganda machine is employing the same tactics it used in Iraq; whether they will lead to the same result, of course, is another matter. Nevertheless, it makes sense that the Bush administration should believe that the United States must back up the worldwide revulsion against its words with worldwide fear of its might.

With its new strategy of the "preemptive strike" buttressed by a defense budget for 2006 of $441 billion, the Bush administration has explicitly linked its imperialist vision with a new militarism. Thus, it should be no surprise that the United States once again leads the world in international arms sales; its profits of about $13 billion—with $8.6 billion coming from arms sales to developing nations—are substantially more than the $5 billion accrued by Russia and the $1 billion by France. Israel has already claimed the right to engage in preemptive strikes, which it did in Syria and Lebanon, and the increasing sale of arms worldwide makes it likely that violence will increase worldwide as well. Such developments can only benefit the most dominant military power, the United States, since new interventions will be required for purposes of "security," and new subservient regimes will be required for purposes of securing stability.

Belief in the need for unilateral action is the logical consequence of such policies, rather than simply an irrational form of machismo. It also follows that the political mind-set of those envisioning new imperial adventures and intensely preparing for war will tend to privilege a mixture of deceit and brutality in foreign affairs. But that is not something the American people can accept without undermining their sense of democratic identity. As partially submerged authoritarian tendencies rise to the surface, Americans become more sensitive to criticism. So, when old allies such as France and Germany opposed the war, they were not simply disagreeing with a policy but expressing their latent hatred for democracy, as well as their jealousy and ingratitude toward the United States.

Democratic interests will be identified with those of the United States, and the interests of the United States will be identified with those of the planet. It doesn't matter whether the United States has the support of most nations or not. If others disagree, they are—by definition—either fools unaware of their real interests or enemies not just of the United States but of humanity as well. Internal opponents of a misguided foreign policy, by the same token, suffer the same fate as old allies with different views. Their goodwill is denied from the start. Critics of the war and the government become "traitors." It follows that the need for vigilance against them must be as unending as the war on terror itself. Obsessive preoccupation with ensuring security and curtailing civil liberties thus becomes a logical extension of new imperialist fantasies rather than simply an expression of irrational paranoia. That all this serves the Bush administration by identifying it with the national interest, and the national interest of the United States with that of the world, apparently remains incomprehensible to the mainstream media. The similarity between the current form of thinking and that of our old communist enemies—who believed that what is good for the party is good for the nation, and what is good for the Soviet Union is good for the world proletariat—is striking.

Again, it is not a matter of this or that policy; it is a matter of the new political agenda and the reactionary ambitions guiding it. The magnitude of the current crisis is still underestimated. What was called the "military-industrial complex" is working to the detriment of the nation. Close to $600 billion of a total budget of $2.6 trillion in 2006 will be devoted to the military. The welfare state, meanwhile, is being stripped to the bone. The same 2006 budget will include cuts or reductions in more than 154 programs that involve public assistance. More than three million jobs have been lost since the new millennium began; about 150,000 jobs would have to be created each month not to recover the jobs already lost but just to keep pace with the current decline. Little is being said about what it would take to counteract these trends in a meaningful way or, to put it differently, to reclaim the antitrust spirit, the New Deal, and the poor people's movement. Mechanically seeking to imitate the Farm and Labor Party or the New Deal or the civil rights movement is insufficient. Determining what they have to offer the core groups of the Democratic Party for a contemporary progressive politics is what needs to be done.

Intoxicated by "the end of ideology," however, the Democrats remain content (as usual) to offer a perspective just a little less loathsome than that of their opponents. They have generally been unwilling to address American gun-running, the economic exploitation of Iraq, and the reality of this new class war. More radical elements might stand in the wings, and perhaps some within the mainstream are reevaluating their positions. Ultimately, however, the call for changes and the pressure to make them must come from outside the ranks of the party. Sources for such pressure exist; huge demonstrations now forgotten bear witness to the depth of dissatisfaction with the status quo, and there exists a colorful mosaic of community organizations, interests groups, and progressive social movements.

Lack of coordination and a common perspective on fighting this new class war is the problem, not simply apathy. Now, more than ever, it is necessary to begin furthering a *class ideal*—a set of values and programs—that speaks to the general interests of working people within each of the existing organizations and movements even as it privileges none. Propagating common values of resistance and articulating new programs of empowerment can occur only by working with the reformist organizations we have; it cannot come from the top down, through sectarian action, or through vague calls for abolishing the system. No longer is it a matter of choosing between reform and revolution. The choice is now between radical reform and resignation. But that choice is no less dramatic. The quality of our future depends on making the right decision.

7

Dub'ya's Fellow Travelers

Left Intellectuals and Mr. Bush's War

Written in collaboration with Kurt Jacobsen

What are "fellow travelers"? Once upon a time, during the 1920s and 1930s, the epithet referred to left-wing intellectuals who, though not members of the Communist Party, were sympathetic to its political project. No preening right-winger or proud moderate will ever let anyone on the Left forget how writers such as Lion Feuchtwanger, Romain Rolland, Lincoln Steffens, and Beatrice and Sidney Webb traipsed off into darkest Russia, went on gracious NKVD-guided tours of the glorious Soviet future, and rhapsodized that, so far as they could see, it worked. Indeed, no one should forget this profoundly pathetic episode. True, many inquisitive visitors, such as André Gide, were deeply shaken by what they experienced there as well. But it spoils all the fun to dwell on those who, in the words of Victor Serge, "had the courage to see clearly."

It's more entertaining to point to those who saw what they wanted to see; trumpeted ideals that lacked any relation to reality; invoked "history" because they understood nothing of the present; and, whatever their good intentions, provided what the communists liked to call an "objective apology"—or what Karl Rove might call good public relations—for an increasingly xenophobic, imperialist, and authoritarian regime. Those naifs of times past should be held strictly accountable. A similar standard should be set, however, for their contemporary left-wing counterparts who endorsed the ideological beliefs that produced the Iraqi War and, in the process, helped legitimate the reactionary Bush administration.

Most of today's fellow travelers hitch rides with the Democratic Party. But whereas it was once assumed that critical intellectuals should aim to illuminate, or expose, the confusions of sly politicians, stand with the more radical spirits on the ground, and push and prod the establishment to the left, these truculent champions of progress adopt the same assumptions and the same fears as the candidates on the stump. In light of what has occurred in Iraq, and in a textbook example of paranoid projection, the fellow travelers now have the chutzpah to inveigh against their critics for supposedly trying to drive them out of the Democratic Party[1]—as if that were possible. Precisely they, and their sort, are the most firmly entrenched. Like the mainstream Democrats, most of Dub'ya's fellow travelers initially supported the war—a smart tactic up to the giddy moment that the president considered it safe to proclaim "mission accomplished!"—and now, shocked and awed by the Iraqi debacle, they shake their heads and ruefully say, "sorry."

Many of these pragmatists, it seems, were woefully misled by (gasp!) false information. Few of them, apparently, could imagine how wretchedly the Iraqi war and occupation would be mishandled. It was also inconceivable to them that the motives of the U.S. government would be anything less than impeccable. Of course, the sobering information was always out there in abundance. There was never a wisp of a reason to trust Commander Bush and his neoconservative Rough Riders. Administration officials such as Richard Perle and Paul Wolfowitz actually admitted publicly to the seamier motives that inspired the invasion. It was always ludicrous to believe that a democratic domino effect would start in conquered Baghdad; that the United States had the right, the reason, and the wisdom to unilaterally pursue a "preventive" war; or that the Iraqi population would welcome the invaders with open arms. Looking at the deteriorating situation now, it is appalling what grisly travesties this loose band of "moderate" social democrats and tepid liberals has aided and abetted; it is even more appalling how little the sway of genuine self-criticism appeals to these self-styled political "realists," most of whom know as little about Middle Eastern politics or Islam as the authors of this piece know about astrophysics or break dancing.

Bush and his surly gang probably couldn't believe their luck at the willing inflow of progressive acolytes, or what Lenin would have called "useful idiots." Finally, here were some mature, responsible, patriotic radicals ready to engage the "mainstream" or, to put it another way, ready to publish and speak and opine supinely in the mainstream media. The Bush boys must have died laughing at these raw recruits who showed so little savvy when the cynical call came to "rally round the flag," who were so susceptible to the official exploitation of fear. Not all the fellow travelers' prior knowledge of the sour realities of "hard-ball" politics, nor the inveterate money-grubbing and power grabbing of the upper tiers, would dissuade them from jumping headfirst into that blurry Huntingtonian universe of clashing civilizations. They never noticed that distinct whiff of the beer-hall putsch that hovered over these feral Republicans whom many embraced as saviors.

Could any sentient human being fall for the sloganeering guff of this slavering saber-toothed pack occupying the White House? Nothing was more mystifying than the improbable Damascan conversion that major figures on the Left underwent as the Twin Towers came tumbling down. Wasn't it crystal clear that, from the start, there was nothing Dub'ya's gang would not use to further their agenda? Come to think of it, isn't that what all politicians at all times are supposed to do with events—turn them to advantage? Did this most elementary truism not dawn on Christopher Hitchens, Paul Berman, Michael Ignatieff, Mitchell Cohen, Todd Gitlin, Michael Walzer, and other skittish strays away from the Left? One suspects that they may have watched too many Hollywood movies in which a national emergency melts class and status lines to climax in the raising of musketeer swords— "all for one and one for all"—for the common good. Or perhaps they were too obsessed with Israel and too distrustful of those categorical "Arabs." Was it really so difficult to see through the endless bullshit shoveled by this administration? You didn't need a weatherman to know which way the wind was blowing, or a veterinarian to diagnose that a rabid bunch of right-wingers was steering the country over the nearest cliff.

These newly minted fellow travelers never dreamed that it could happen to *them*. The paragon pundits always believed that it was only the radicals and the ultraleftists who were eager to embrace hero cults and orchestrated deceits. But the Republican Party—incarnating Bob Dylan's "superhuman crew who go out and round up everyone that knows more than they do"—was just waiting for the suckers. And this new batch was happy to oblige. *They* weren't lunatics like Noam Chomsky or part of that nameless crowd who supposedly expressed "glee" that the United States got what it deserved on 9/11,[2] but rather mature, responsible, and—always conveniently—patriotic.

What is the problem with Chomsky anyway? That he writes a lot of books? That the kids love him? That he has been uncompromising in confronting the Goliath? That even his mistakes are bold? That he is far more often right than wrong? That he was a critic of Israeli territorial ambitions while many of its left-wing supporters were still dreaming of milk and honey? No one views him as an infallible prophet. But the fellow travelers seem obsessed with him. Certain of them, in fact, see the need to situate their milquetoast position "between" Cheney and Chomsky,[3] as if, in the muddled realm of their own private world spirit, it makes sense to juxtapose a *vice president*—whose influence is paramount and whose clique has produced both the current catastrophe and an almost unimaginable decline in the worldwide standing of the United States—and a *professor at MIT*—who has long been outcast by the ideological mainstream and has no institutional influence whatsoever. Calling on the Left to position itself between Cheney and Chomsky is possible only by ignoring the existing power relations. But wait (silly us!); that's not quite true. What results from this frisky exercise in critical analysis is yet another stale and salable vision of a "liberal foreign policy" totally amenable to the Democratic Leadership Council.

What is it about Chomsky? Even Adam Shatz of the *Nation*,[4] who really ought to know better, accused him of "evaluating the war through the prism of anti-Americanism" by spending too little time on the assault staged by the followers of bin Laden and too much on the atrocities sponsored by the United States. A supercilious argument like that of Todd Gitlin, which rests on the belief that "the tone *was* the position," doesn't exactly amount to a palpable reason for burning Chomsky at the stake. Apparently, if you strike the right reverential tone, you can say anything. The MIT maverick is just not sensitive enough to appreciate that "patriotism is not only a gift to others, it is a self-declaration. It affirms that who you are extends beyond—far beyond—yourself, or the limited being that you thought was yourself." Very deep.

Snap off a salute to gung-ho Gitlin! Because *he* hung Old Glory from his terrace in New York on 9/11, in what was surely hostile terrain rife with traitors and Islamic sympathizers, future generations will undoubtedly be better able to savor his thrilling insight that "lived patriotism entails sacrifice."[5] Not that *his* action should be construed as providing "support for the policies of George Bush." Oh, no. But let us not forget that this is the same stalwart who, in his *Letters to a Young Activist,* called the McCarthy witch hunt "a mixed blessing," urged leftists to hunt down "Islamic murderers," and preached that there is no salvation outside the Democrats no matter how far to the right they scurry. Members of the chorus cheering on Mr. Bush's foreign policy were probably driven crazy by Chomsky's insistence on viewing the attacks of 9/11 as a "crime against humanity" rather than an act of war—even though, of course, bin Laden represented no particular nation or people. But that is obviously a mere technicality.

So what do these latter-day fellow travelers offer instead? A standpoint that perfectly suits a Democratic Party whose presidential candidate presented himself as the second coming of General George Patton, the proponent of even more funds for an infinitely centralized homeland security apparatus, and—just before smelly things started going completely down the toilet—a belated opponent of the Iraqi war. No less than Gitlin, other fellow travelers have plenty of pompous advice to offer. They want to make sure that the rest of us recognize the crying need to make judgments and not fall into hopeless relativism, "because the refusal to make judgments is fundamentally undemocratic and fundamentally apolitical."[6] Did Allan Bloom climb out of his coffin? Thanks for that.

It would be nice to know just who constitutes this ubiquitous Left that the fellow travelers beat up on so valiantly. Well, of course, there's Chomsky. But then, he can be accused of every sin known to humankind with carefree impunity. Who else? We tend to doubt that "judgments" are evaded, that "relativism" rules, and that "third worldism" is the rage among the bulk of writers for journals such as *In These Times, Mother Jones, New Politics, New Political Science, Science and Society, Theory and Society, Logos, Counterpunch, Z-Net,* or any other leftist outlet with a serious constituency. But unfortunately, just what political judgments the Left should make—other than heed the advice of Michael Walzer and surrender its allegedly implacable third worldism, confess that the United States is not the sole bastion of "evil," and recognize the all-absolving character of the "new" situation for the United States—always remains a bit foggy.

Luckily, our fellow travelers know what's up. Michael Walzer and Jean Elshtain got a firm grip on the situation when they signed the war manifesto "What We're Fighting For,"[7] sponsored by the center-right Institute for American Values. It stands for "freedom," and if the document explicitly equates freedom with the American understanding of it, no big deal. It is enough that the signatories denounced the taking of life, urged aggressive self-defense, and, after the posturing was done, banished any nagging suspicion that the crisis of 9/11 might be manipulated for imperialist purposes. Elshtain goes a step further. She primly alerts us to the seductive dangers of "appeasement," ridicules the notion that any change in U.S. policy will improve the situation, sternly informs us that the world is, you know, a dangerous place, and insists that the "humanist" preference for negotiating with fundamentalist fanatics—not, of course, the Israeli or Saudi or Louisiana sort—is fruitless.[8]

We never heard any of that stuff before. It's always nice to encounter brash new arguments about the need to take up "the burden of American power in a violent world." Silly cynics might wonder whether this dainty counsel amounts to a resurrection of the "white man's burden." Pay them no heed. No "realist" with liberal principles would ever abide the idea that foreign policy might have a racist component. It does seem strange that the enemy du jour of the United States always seems to be a people of color or a nation with little taste for its brand of globalization. But, never mind.

It is interesting how the signatories to the rousing "What We're Fighting For"—half of whom are conservative enough to actually join the present administration—never bothered to consider that perhaps the fanatics are less enraged by the way Americans live in their own country than by the policies the U.S. government pursues in the Islamic world. Like Elshtain, however, Walzer was probably contemplating higher things like the theory of "just war" and the ethical obligation to "reconstruct" what has been destroyed. Not that he was ardently supportive of the Iraqi invasion. Walzer cheered the first Gulf War of 1991 to save Kuwait from the clutches of Saddam,[9] though Kuwait was never exactly a shining ideal of democracy, but he has said any number of different things at different times about the second Gulf War. The stance of our hero is, shall we say, nuanced.

Ever the hand-wringing Democrat, to be sure, Walzer recognized that the administration of Bush the Younger never made its clinching case for the invasion of Iraq.[10] In spite of that, however, the war had to be supported—sort of. Though the American presence is only stoking the chaos and the majority of Iraqis want us out of their country, Walzer believes that it is ethically incumbent on us to reconstruct this nation that we are so intent on devastating.[11] Is the reader following this lucid argument? Let's try again. The war on terror should not excuse "indefensible" policies, although, given a state of "supreme emergency,"[12] an "emergency ethics" may be required, even if it provides no criteria for either judging which policies are defensible or examining the interests of those in whose name the policies are undertaken. Still don't get it?

One more time: Since a war is being fought against terror in the name of liberal principles under ill-defined emergency conditions, it might be legitimate on ethical grounds to consider employing military courts and constricting civil liberties, which violate those same liberal principles.[13] Okay, since these are "complex" arguments, let's cut to the chase. Mature and responsible and patriotic left-wing intellectuals should tell the Bushies: "Do what you gotta do, and in the name of the national security and what Gore Vidal calls 'perpetual war for perpetual peace,' we'll hold our noses and support you." Or, if that doesn't fly, we'll retreat into the great dusty documents of liberal Zionism and ponder deeply the reasons why its venerated values have eroded.

As for Mitchell Cohen, editor of *Dissent,* who knows what he was thinking when he made the feverish claim that those who refused to support the invasion of Iraq surely would have stood aside in 1941 as well. His tender little missive, "The Real, Not the Comfortable Choice,"[14] harked back to the Baghdad of 1941 and the specter of pogroms envisioned by the notorious anti-Jewish bigot Rashid Ali. There's nothing like the good old days! And, with them in mind, heady dreams of regime change can be transported into the present. Justifications abound: Cohen highlights the hideous character of Saddam's regime, castigates the hamstrung UN for its "many failures," insists on the sky-is-falling peril posed by Saddam, calls for a democratic Iraq, advocates turning the UN into "an effective institution with real integrity" (by which he seems to mean a marionette of the United States), and emphasizes that the choice is not between "war and peace but, absent an unlikely coup in Baghdad—the use of force "sooner or later." [15] It's remarkable, isn't it, how he gets to the core of what is at stake?

There is not one word about the constraints, the potential costs, or the regional implications of an invasion. And Mitch, believe it or not, 2004 is not 1941: there is no world war, and there is no Hitler for whom Saddam is acting in proxy. Everyone now knows—just as many knew even before the bombings began—that Saddam posed no threat to the security of the United States and that ridding Iraq of the mustachioed monster through invasion would produce national resistance, a spur for real terrorists, a spate of anti-Americanism, and even greater chaos in the region. It was never a question of war now or war later. State Department and intelligence analysts realized from the start that none of the guys we backed was in it for democracy, including those American stooges in exile Ahmed Chalabi and Ayed al-Allawi, who played their neoconservative cronies for first-class fools. Democracy? Whatever happened to the emirs in Kuwait? Still in charge? Our slick fellow travelers apparently never bothered to consider the vulgar notion that this war was being fought for oil, for water, for military bases outside Saudi Arabia, and to provide a tart warning to other states in the region—which Libya quickly understood—of what would happen if they did not toe the American line. Not to worry. No facile anti-Americanism, dogmatic Marxism, or anachronistic theories of imperialism would ever seduce our hardy fellow travelers!

When we visited Iraq with a peace delegation in January 2003 (see chapter 3) we helped draw up an antiwar statement that both opposed the war and rejected Saddam Hussein.[16] As soon as we returned, we worked with many others on the Left to expose the lies and the false assumptions deployed by the Bush administration in favor of invasion.[17] Efforts of this sort were studiously ignored, or even condemned, in the mainstream media, on cue, by many of Dub'ya's fellow travelers. A petition was distributed that got 33,000 signatories. *Everyone* sensed disaster in the making. The Internet was bursting with warnings, various military leaders and even the CIA advised caution, the much-maligned United Nations knew that Colin Powell was shilling for his boss, and the rest of the world realized that Bush the Younger and his gun-slinging gang had gone more than slightly nuts.

According to Dub'ya's fellow travelers, however, the critics—and especially those teeming demonstrators all over the world—were misguided idiots. Not that the erudite editors of *Dissent* and the *New Republic* weren't trying to set them straight, mind you. Our new *politerati* were probably learning at the feet of Michael Lind, a one-time conservative who allegedly lurched left and realized the importance of embracing that always elusive center; they were learning that the Vietnam War was actually well worth fighting[18] and understanding that there was no need to worry about the endemic tendency of refreshingly mature, responsible, and patriotic social democrats to make fools of themselves by blessing imperialist wars waged in the fig-leaf name of humanitarian ideals.

One wonders: Did the fellow travelers—souls of political practicality—really swallow the soothing bromides that men like Bush "grow in office" or "rise to the occasion" or some other outright miracle? Or were they intimidated into their display of stunted, smarmy patriotism? What motivated these new cheerleaders? Was it really a "theocratic fascist" threat to the world's mightiest superpower, always the innocent, that scared them? Or did a yen for protective coloration play a role? Let there be no misunderstanding: Reasonable disagreements can exist on the Left. They were in evidence before the bombing of Serbia and over the need for a powerful response against the crimes of 9/11 by Osama bin Laden and the Taliban. But there is no sane reason why support for the attack on Afghanistan had to turn into unqualified support for a war without end and preemptive strikes against any nation defined as an enemy by some whim of the Bush administration.[19] Instead of promoting an alternative foreign policy to punish the criminal act of 9/11 by concentrating on capturing Osama bin Laden and rebuilding Afghanistan, or explaining how the war in Iraq was the second front in a right-wing assault on the welfare state, our fellow travelers were simply content to rubber- stamp the basic beliefs underpinning a neoconservative foreign policy.

Christopher Hitchens is the most spectacular case. He is also the least apologetic. The former secretary of the Oxford University Labor Club, who grew up amid the sectarian strife on the British Left, humbly insists that history is always on his side. He is a terrific essayist and a remarkably intelligent man, a writer who took on Henry Kissinger and Mother Teresa, and one still nurses a faint hope that he'll snap out of it. One of us watched Hitchens in Chicago, just prior to the invasion, skillfully fencing with various dreary sectarian interrogators in the audience, which was fair enough and well deserved, but Hitchens dealt just as viciously with plainly "civilian" questioners. Some folks, like overtrained "killing machine" soldiers, just can't turn it off. Their own acuity gets in the way of reality.

Maybe that is the problem. Hitchens, in an essay on a Whittaker Chambers, once chidingly wrote: "The Cold War was fought just as hard in France or Germany or England, but without the same grotesque paranoia or the chilling readiness to surrender liberty and believe the absurd [as in the United States during the McCarthy era]."[20] Hey, no kidding? Chambers's tragedy is that he ultimately lent "himself to the most depraved right-wing circles, whose real objective is the undoing of the New Deal and the imposition of a politically conformist America." One fervently hopes that Hitchens rereads his earlier works; they might spark some curative self-reflection.

For sure, this recent convert to Bushism can still sling it with the best and worst of them. Hitchens's *Long Short War* rails at those who "do not think that Saddam Hussein is a bad guy at all."

It notes how those who protested the war were nothing but "blithering ex-flower child[ren] or ranting neo-Stalinist[s]." All the critics are beneath contempt; the need for an Iraqi invasion was self-evident, and if the policy hasn't worked, then surely "history" will, sometime or other, make it turn out right. Just after 9/11, Hitchens wrote in the *Nation* that U.S. forces' reluctance to carpet bomb Afghanistan showed "an almost pedantic policy of avoiding 'collateral damage.'" Maybe the warping began then. And, he opined, any effort to understand the sources of terrorism can only "rationalize" it. What sort of intellectual tells other people what is fit to think about? Though one may wonder at times whether Hitchens has literally lost his mind, it is still in many respects one to be reckoned with.

We keep remembering the old Hitchens. Take his zesty essay on Isaiah Berlin, which undermines Michael Ignatieff's reverential take on the crusty old boy, a vain if exceptionally erudite fellow given to justifying Zionism and hanging around during the Vietnam War with the likes of the Bundys, William and McGeorge, perhaps because Sir Isaiah liked playing tough guy.[21] It is the same with his acolyte. There are plenty of times to be tough, but the question is when to put up those fists. Ignatieff understands the need for restraint; his concern with maintaining civil liberties, or tipping the scale toward maintaining them even when confronted with emergency situations, is real.[22] He is committed to the liberal rule of law and is willing to take on the Bush administration for its refusal to extend judicial review to supposed terrorists or terrorist supporters. All this makes even more bizarre his decision to endorse Bush's escapades based on the fantastic notion that "liberal interventionism"—led by the virtuous United States, whether or not in conformity with international law, and with or without backing from the United Nations—can save the world from itself.

Ignatieff justified his decision by referring to Saddam's

abysmal record on human rights, the possibility of changing the balance of power in the region by toppling Saddam, and anxiety over the possibility of Saddam getting nuclear weapons in the future.[23] What differentiates his support of the Iraqi war from his opposition to the Vietnam War, however, is really nothing more than efficacy.[24] None of the reasons Ignatieff provides for extending support to Bush can stand up to the most elementary political reflection: Saddam was a tyrant, but that does not justify contravening international law; Iraq was never the most dominant power in the region; and one does not unleash the winds of war in the name of what might occur some unspecified number of years down the road. Probably something else was at stake. In the *New York Times,* reflecting the febrile verities of Rudyard Kipling, Ignatieff stated that the Persian Gulf is "the empire's center of gravity," where the United States must take up "the burden of empire."[25] Now, of course, he too is sorry. Though we won't know whether the war was worth it for any number of years—note the contradiction with the thinking used to justify the invasion—it was clearly not carried out properly to his strategic satisfaction.

Let's not forget Paul Berman. For this decorated veteran of the 1960s who has turned into a solid citizen while fighting for space in the *New York Times,* it seems that, following 9/11, the "entire situation had the look of Europe in 1939." When in doubt, follow the demagogue and drag in Hitler; it may be a red herring, but what the hell, the tactic always works. Anyway, upon sagacious reflection, Berman, despite calling Bush "the worst president the US ever had," undauntedly reached the conclusion that the new imperialism "is not a pure power grab; it is not designed to control territory." After all, in spite of America's ostentatiously mixed motives, there are "many peoples who owe their freedom to an exercise of American military power."

Well, perhaps Bush really invaded Iraq to save its museums and libraries from the loutish locals. Ignatieff likewise says that, whatever the impure intentions and the mistakes of the United States, it would be unfair to "discredit its humanitarian ideals."[26] But of course, there are also mass graves dotting the planet, from El Salvador to Indonesia, that wouldn't need to have been dug except for American interference. Or have they simply, pardon the expression, disappeared? In any event, under the banner of "a liberal's war of liberation," the intrepid radical Berman let no opportunity slip to deride those prissy leftists who "worried about America's imperial motives, about the greed of big corporations, and their influence in White House policy; and could not get beyond their worries."[27] How narrow the thinking of those leftists was. Never mind how things are turning out for the Iraqis living under an occupier: their infrastructure is destroyed, their nation is ecologically devastated, unemployment is soaring, health services are virtually nonexistent, gang warfare is being carried on in the streets, their major cities and most revered mosques are in ruins, their government lacks legitimacy, more than 100,000 are dead, and no one really knows—or, in the American heartland, probably cares—how many more are crippled and wounded.[28] All of this is surely a matter of collateral damage and well worth the price that the Iraqis—not, of course, the fellow travelers—must pay for freedom.

What on earth were these high-IQ dupes thinking? That a Bush-led "crusade" would stamp out religious fundamentalism around the world and maybe even at Bob Jones University too? A pervasive plight, or ploy, is the one that John Kerry got himself into with his waffling reply that, knowing what he knows now, he would have authorized Bush's war, but not necessarily Bush's actions. This dense mix of stubborn defensiveness and sly arrogance is hard to penetrate. Everyone makes mistakes. But the difference is that when managers and coaches make mistakes and their teams suffer losses, they get fired; our unctuous pseudo-left-wing pundits are rewarded with yet another gig to explain why everything would have been all right if only those fools in office had done it differently and to justify a set of explanations that made no sense then and make even less sense now.

"Few things are more dangerous," as Eric Hobsbawm observed, "than empires pursuing their own interest in the belief that they are doing humanity a favour." Likewise, few things are as preposterous as liberal and leftist intellectuals who ride media shotgun for them. And in the name of what: belief in a "just war"? Hundreds of billions of dollars and thousands of lives have been wasted in a war that was obviously "necessary" only to those who are now comfortably sitting in their offices and pontificating about the need for young people to be mature, responsible, and patriotic so as not to piss off the "undecided" vote that ultimately slipped away in any case.

It is nice to see that our fellow travelers have not shied away from taking a strong stand—and on such intelligent grounds. Seriously, though, it is precisely these people who could have had a positive impact on the Left and the Democratic Party. Almost all the fellow travelers are well-known public intellectuals associated with venerable journals such as *Dissent* and the *New Republic* that, traditionally, have acted as gadflys among the more left-wing elements of the political mainstream. But that time is now long past. Our fellow travelers aren't interested in building a critical consciousness anymore. Quite the contrary: they actually helped create the ideological climate in which the Bush administration could thrive and, in the process, gave its policies the type of intellectual cachet they did not deserve. This hindered the development of an alternative agenda. Looking down on the people in the streets while fawning over the Democrats in office, completely blind to the ideological onslaught of the Right, these political pundits remained content to justify the compromises and vacillations associated with winning over what Arthur Schlesinger, Jr. once termed "the vital center." It is pathetic how far removed these fellow travelers are from the reality they claim to judge with such arrogance and authority. With their platitudes and cheap realism, they contribute to the further decline of what was once an estimable political culture of the Left.

8

Constructing Neoconservatism

Neoconservatism has become a code word for reactionary thinking in our time and a badge of unity for those in the Bush administration advocating a new imperialist foreign policy, an assault on the welfare state, and a return to "family values." Its members are directly culpable for the disintegration of American prestige abroad, the erosion of a huge budget surplus, and the debasement of democracy at home. Iraq has turned into a disaster, and much of the American citizenry has been revolted by the arrogance, lies, and incompetence of leading neoconservatives within the administration. But their agenda remains fixed; the alternative has not been adequately articulated. Mainstream media still take the intellectual pretensions of neoconservative ideologues far too seriously and treat them far too courteously. Their arguments, especially in the realm of foreign policy, are actually quite elementary. The unassailable superiority of American values makes their extension throughout the world necessary; this, in turn, requires radically increasing "defense" spending, introducing measures capable of building national unity, ignoring incompetent international organizations, and insisting on the right to intervene unilaterally whenever and wherever the government believes it must.[1] These arguments require blunt responses, and future activists require a sense of the truly bizarre character of this mafia. Thus, there is a need for what might be termed a rough montage of its principal intellectuals and activists.

Secretary of Defense Donald Rumsfeld and his former deputy secretary Paul Wolfowitz require no introduction. These architects of the Iraqi war misled the American public about the existence of weapons of mass destruction, the horrible pattern of torturing prisoners of war, the connection (or lack thereof) between Saddam Hussein and al Qaeda, the resistance that would greet the invading troops, the difficulty of setting up a democracy in Iraq, and the threat Iraq supposedly posed to the United States. But Rumsfeld and Wolfowitz remain unrepentant. Whispering words of encouragement was the notorious Richard Perle, director of the Defense Policy Board until his resignation amid accusations of conflict of interest. His nickname, the "prince of darkness," reflects his advanced views on nuclear weapons. Advice was also forthcoming from Elliott Abrams. Pardoned by George Bush the Elder in 1991 after being found guilty of lying to Congress during the Iran-contra scandal, Abrams is now in charge of Middle Eastern affairs; he remains an admirer of the witch hunts led by Senator Joseph McCarthy. Also of interest is John Bolton, former undersecretary of state for disarmament and perhaps future ambassador to the UN, who has little use for either arms control or international law. Then there is our Bible-thumping former attorney general John Ashcroft, who is rumored to speak in tongues and whose face has graced the cover of the official journal of the National Rifle Association.

But others also deserve mention. Chairman of the Republican Party—also known as "Bush's pit bull"—Ed Gillespie is a protégé of the arch-reactionary Dick Armey, former House majority leader. As for the current ideological leader of Republicans in the House of Representatives, Tom DeLay (R-Tex.), a particular favorite of Enron and affectionately known as the "hammer," once likened the Environmental Protection

Agency to the Gestapo. In the Senate, meanwhile, Rick Santorum (R-Pa.) has opposed abolishing laws forbidding sodomy, since he feels this would open the way to lifting laws on incest and the like. It is instructive to note that such neoconservatives helped foil the reelection bid of former senator Max Cleland (R-Ga.)— who lost three limbs in Vietnam—because he was apparently not patriotic enough. Within the Oval Office, staunch neoconservatives such as Vice President Dick Cheney and his assistant I. Lewis ("Scooter") Libby, as well as Presidential Chief of Staff Karl Rove, are among the closest advisers to President Bush.

Neoconservatism also has its intellectuals. Journals such as the *Public Interest,* formerly edited by Irving Kristol (also known as the "godfather"), and *Commentary,* formerly edited by Norman Podhoretz, framed neoconservatism's general outlook on issues ranging from the need for new censorship laws and the importance of reasserting the capitalist ethos to the lack of anticommunist vigor on the part of Albert Camus and George Orwell. The wife of Podhoretz, Midge Decter, is the adoring biographer of Rumsfeld and the busy defender of Israel; Gertrude Himmelfarb, the noted historian and wife of Kristol, is a champion of organized religion and the Victorians. Their offspring are also carrying on the tradition: John Podhoretz is a columnist for the tabloid *New York Post,* which is owned by the notorious Rupert Murdoch, who also employs William Kristol as editor of the *Weekly Standard.* Other neoconservative intellectuals include the editor of the *New Criterion,* Hilton Kramer, whose time is spent bemoaning the decline of cultural standards and whose literary tastes are so straight that they creak. Then, too, there is our former "drug czar," the posturing and self-righteous author of *The Book of Virtues,* William J. Bennett, who recently admitted to having somewhat of a gambling problem, and Dinesh D'Souza, who has comforted us all by celebrating "the end of racism."

Neoconservatism can be identified with a small network of influential intellectuals and friends whose thinking originated in the anticommunist Committee on the Present Danger of 1950, which in 1997 made way for the Project for a New American Century.[2] But the ideology has supporters with far broader appeal. Serious publications such as the *Wall Street Journal* reach the "opinion makers." Hack columnists such as Steve Dunleavy, Michelle Caulkin, and Maggie Gallagher, associated with the *New York Post* and other tabloids, popularize neoconservative ideas. Radio hosts Bob Grant, Rush Limbaugh, Michael Savage, and Laura Schlesinger add fuel to the fire by ranting against traitors, fundamentalists, and sexual perverts. Even more important in this regard are the television pundits—Anne Coulter, Bill O'Reilly, Jerry Falwell, and Pat Robertson—who gather around reactionary networks like Fox. The pandering of these media thugs to the lowest ideological common denominator, their unwillingness to engage an argument, and their bullying arrogance perfectly express a neoconservative sensibility that teeters on the edge of fascism.

A no-nonsense attitude informs the neoconservative outlook; its advocates strike the tough-guy pose all the time. Their intimidating style tends to deflect attention from their paucity of ideas and the ultimately contradictory interests they claim to represent. Identifying these ideas and interests remains important, however, both for understanding the current political landscape and for contesting the contemporary forces of reaction. What is unique about neoconservatism, compared with more traditional forms of conservatism, requires specification, especially because this new version of reactionary thought is far more lethal and vulgar than that of its establishmentarian predecessors.

Roots

Old-fashioned conservatism actually derives less from political than from cultural assumptions. The preeminent conservative philosopher of our time, Michael Oakeshott, saw this philosophy as resting on a certain psychological "disposition" to favor the unadventurous and the already established over the new and the untried.[3] To be sure, this disposition places conservatism in a somewhat ambivalent relationship to capitalism. It is obviously the established economic system, but it is also dynamic and contemptuous of parochial and provincial customs. Capitalism is fueled by technological progress, and it is intent on breaking down what Marx termed "the Chinese walls of tradition" and reducing all venerable relations to "the cash nexus." This rubs against the grain of those who fear, with Edmund Burke, that "the fine draperies of life" are being ripped asunder. But it is incumbent for the worldly-wise conservative to face "reality." He or she is always ruefully willing to admit that the "old world" is being left behind. A dash of cultural pessimism serves as a tonic; it helps create nostalgia for times past.

Conservatism is predicated on a resistance to change. Should reforms or innovations be introduced, however, they must be integrated into the texture of the old and the established as quickly and as smoothly as possible. This desire enables conservatives to turn necessity into a virtue. Because any reform *can* become part of our heritage, at least in principle, conservatives *can* adapt to any change. They can even take credit for being flexible and negotiating the connection between past and future. So, even though prejudice and an elitist sensibility have always been important elements of traditional conservative thought, modern conservatives can now—though somewhat grudgingly—condemn all forms of prejudice.

That their intellectual and political predecessors vociferously opposed the civil rights movements and the new social movements is irrelevant. Conservatives are parasitic. They place themselves in the position of the "free rider," or the individual who, though refusing to take the initiative on any reform, will—graciously, if somewhat skeptically—adapt to the changes brought about by others. Being stubborn flies in the face of the conservative disposition. Stability and continuity are its primary concerns. The crux of the matter is clear enough: "he who lives in comfort," wrote Bertolt Brecht, "lives comfortably."

Neoconservatism begins with different premises. Some of its staunchest advocates, such as Perle and Wolfowitz, originally met and became friends at the University of Chicago, where they attended seminars given by Albert Wohlstetter, mathematician and senior staff member at the Rand Corporation. A few, such as Allan Bloom, translator of Plato and author of *The Closing of the American Mind,* were influenced by the writings of the important political philosopher Leo Strauss at the University of Chicago.[4] But neoconservatism actually has little in common with his attempt to develop an intellectual "aristocracy" capable of preserving the classical tradition in a "mass democracy." No less than Plato, perhaps, neoconservatives may think that they are employing the "noble lie." But their form of lying is far more banal than the attempt of this great thinker to veil his lack of philosophical foundations for an ideal state. Neoconservatives employ their mendacity like any ordinary group of liars: to justify this interest or cover up that mistake.

Leo Strauss may have argued that political philosophy went into decline with Machiavelli and the erosion of a religious universe.[5] Unlike his supposed followers, however, Strauss was essentially unconcerned with the practical imperatives of "realism," let alone the cruder variety. He surely would have cringed at the fashionable attempt to suggest that American foreign policy is indebted to the realism of Thomas Hobbes, while that of Europe is mired in the idealism of Immanuel Kant.[6] The writings of neoconservatives generally evidence little interest in the "conversation" between classical authors, textual exegesis, or intellectual nuance in general. The influence of conservative political philosophy on the neoconservative mandarins is overrated. Those preoccupied with it only lend an air of intellectualism to what is little more than a brutal reliance on power and propaganda.

Neoconservatives lack the complacent disposition, the elitist *longeur*, the respect for established hierarchies, the fear of change, and the staid preoccupation with stability of the more traditional conservatives. Their resentment of intellectuals, no less than their cultural tastes, recalls the "good old boy." Neoconservatives are unconcerned with strengthening the ties that should bind—using another telling phrase from Burke— "the dead, the living, and the yet unborn." They are revolutionaries or, better, counterrevolutionaries intent on remaking America. Just as the avant-garde composer-hero of *Doctor Faustus* by Thomas Mann was obsessed with rolling back the most progressive achievement of modern music, Beethoven's Ninth Symphony, so is the neoconservative vanguard obsessed with rolling back the most progressive political achievements of the last century.

More important than the influence of traditional conservatism is the simple anticommunism learned by many elder statesmen of neoconservatism when they were youthful Trotskyists. There is a sense in which Irving Kristol, Norman Podhoretz, and others remain defined by the communist dogmatism they sought to oppose. The virtue of the party or clique—*their* party or clique–needs no complex justification; it stands for the interests of the revolution or, in this instance, democracy. Truth matters little, and morality, other than the morality of unquestioning allegiance to the given political project, matters less. Neoconservatives share with Mao Tse-tung the belief that power comes from the barrel of a gun and, like the commissars of old, that critics are merely providing an objective apology for the enemies of freedom.

Interestingly, the political outlook of future neoconservatives in the 1960s was remarkably like that of the influential senator Henry "Scoop" Jackson (D-Wash.). They too were vehemently anticommunist and strong on defense, accepting of the civil rights movement, and supportive of welfare state policies associated with the New Deal. They began, in short, neither as "know-nothing" populists nor as principled advocates of the free market. Criticism of social movements began with the emergence of black nationalism, concern over the growth of anti-Semitism, and left-wing criticism of Israel. Only during the Reagan administration, however, would it become necessary to choose between "guns" and "butter." Support for social movements and the welfare state thus melted away until, finally, a genuinely radical stance congealed, which was intent on abolishing the most progressive achievements of the century in terms of state action, foreign policy, civil liberties, and cultural freedom.

Neoconservatives today are engaged in an assault on a tradition of social reform extending from Theodore Roosevelt's attack on trusts and the onerous practices of corporations to the New Deal, with its socialist reliance on "big government," and the complex of programs associated with the Great Society of Lyndon Johnson. Neoconservatism also wishes to contest a democratic and cosmopolitan vision of foreign policy that ranges from the beginnings of international law and the Enlightenment, to the critique of "secret diplomacy" by Marx, to the support for international institutions provided by

Woodrow Wilson and FDR, to the current struggle for human rights. In the eyes of neoconservatives, the United States is a society that is always under siege. It has no room for the one who thinks differently; liberty is something that each American supposedly possesses but none—other than the most righteous and most patriotic—should ever exercise. These attitudes, indeed, run deep among certain elements of the American public.

Neoconservatives insisted from the start on a muscular anticommunist foreign policy and a critique of détente, arms control, and the language of idealism. But they have proved willing to use the language of human rights when necessary and to cloak their policies in the rhetoric of democracy. Often the ploy worked; it undoubtedly helped seduce various high-minded liberals such as Michael Ignatieff and Paul Berman into supporting the invasion of Iraq. Such ideals, however, have generally been valued only in the breach. Most neoconservatives made their reputations as "realists." Foreign policy analysts who consider themselves Machiavellian realists, such as Michael Ledeen, have little use for the naive preoccupation with human rights, just as domestic policy analysts such as Charles Murray care little about the do-gooders whose use of the state to intervene in the economy supposedly only worsens the conditions of working people and the poor.[7] It is still the case that most disillusioned former supporters of the Iraqi war contest not the enterprise itself but rather the way it was conducted.

Neoconservatism is, however, not simply concerned with foreign policy. Its representatives view with despair what they consider the erosion of America as a white, male, straight society; their special target is what Norman Podhoretz originally termed an "adversary culture" of the 1960s.[8] Neoconservatives wish to institute a new respect for traditional political authority, capitalism, and the entire complex of concerns associated with "family values." These are perhaps best expressed in the television shows of the 1950s and early 1960s: *Father Knows Best, Leave It to Beaver, My Three Sons, Ozzie and Harriet,* and the rest. The "other" never made an appearance: women were in the kitchen, blacks doffed their caps, and homosexuality did not exist. Nostalgia tends to erase public memories of the lives ruined and the talents squandered in that world of parochialism and prejudice.

The new architects of reaction understand that the trauma associated with 1968 transcends the humiliation created by a lost war, a vice president who barely avoided imprisonment on charges of bribery, and the resignation of a president who clearly was a "crook." Since that time, the government and what President Eisenhower termed the "military-industrial complex" must count on *public* skepticism from its citizens with respect to its motives and policies. What in the 1950s was seemingly a culture of contentment and passivity was transformed during the 1960s into a new culture that was critical of the "silent majority" and no longer complacent in its assumptions about what Daniel Bell termed "the end of ideology." New social movements called on middle-class citizens to look at history in a new way; they decried platitudes justifying the policies of elite interests, demanded institutional accountability, and sought a new appreciation for what Montesquieu termed "the spirit of the laws." All this, in keeping with the tenets of neoconservatism, is still seen by much of the broader public as part of what undermined the United States' power and the self-confidence of its citizens. Masses can still be mobilized against the legacy of the new social movements; their achievements should not be taken for granted. The genuine grief expressed following the death of Ronald Reagan was more than the artificial product of a media spectacle.

Inspirations

It is hard to believe that the old man, so sick and senile in the last decade of his life, held his head so high when he entered the presidency during what was the equivalent of a coronation ceremony. His critics liked to make light of him during the 1980s. They snickered when he fell asleep at meetings, joked about his intellect, and rolled their eyes at his policy proposals. While the Left was laughing, however, Ronald Reagan was making a revolution by transforming the foreign policy, the domestic priorities, and the ideological agenda of the United States. His administration had little use for backdoor diplomacy, arms control, and the old policy of containment. President Reagan dared the Soviet Union to compete with his militarism, which it foolishly chose to do; he heightened tensions and spending with defense plans like the "Star Wars" project, intervened repeatedly in Latin America, and showed his lack of concern for legal niceties when it came to scandals such as Iran-contra. The most influential contemporary neoconservatives cut their teeth under Reagan, and it is worth pointing out that when push came to shove in the contested election of 2000, it was his former secretary of state, George Schultz, and his former chief of staff and secretary of the treasury, James Baker, who were calling the shots for George W. Bush.

The Reagan administration insisted on an outrageous military budget and, in conjunction with the introduction of new tax incentives for the rich and "supply-side" economics, created huge deficits, thereby setting the agenda for cutting the welfare state. The economic practice of this administration stood in sharp contrast to its theoretical insistence on lowering the deficit. The presidency of Ronald Reagan also began the assault on unions, community groups, and those whom he termed "special interests." Women were thrown on the defensive with the attack on abortion and the practice of equality. The race card was played in launching a war against affirmative action and social programs directed toward the poor and people of color. Union membership also dwindled in the 1980s, or what is still characterized as the "me decade" and the "decade of greed." Platitudes abounded. The slogan "just say no" may not have had much of an impact in the war on drugs, but it was the first salvo in the fight for "family values." The buck stopped—and started—with Ronald Reagan. He secured the political foundations for the triumph of the neoconservative ideology by forging an alliance between two factions that had traditionally been at war within the reactionary camp.

One faction was composed primarily of elites who were opposed, from the standpoint of principle and interest, to state intervention in the market. Its members basically cared little about the verities associated with "community" or "family values." They became the champions of "globalization" and a version of civil liberties intent on liberating business from regulation. The best intellectual arguments of this reactionary camp derived from Milton Friedman, Friedrich von Hayek, and Robert Nozick.[9] Its public face was best represented, however, by near-forgotten politicians such as Robert Taft and Barry Goldwater. Essentially, this faction of the neoconservative constituency was reactionary in the sense that it wished to return to the old capitalist belief in what C. B. MacPherson termed "possessive individualism" in order to challenge collectivist theories of society in general and socialism in particular.

The other faction has its roots in the "know-nothing" populism of the nineteenth century. Its members have always been prone to nationalist hysteria, traditional prejudices, and parochial values. These are the preachers of fire and brimstone, the Babbitts, the Klansmen without hoods, those on the wrong side of the Scopes trial who turned into adherents of creationism,

and the residual supporters of McCarthyism. Out of this caul-
dron came the religious fundamentalists and Christian Zionists
longingly looking backward to a small-town way of life that never
existed.[10] Obsessed with tradition and conformity, fearful of radical change and any encounter with the "other," these half-baked
communitarians have no use for feminism, identity politics, or
gay rights. But that is not to say that they necessarily oppose
social legislation that benefits working people (so long as the
privileged workers are white). The neoconservative base hates
the intellectual and economic elites, or what is often referred
to as the "eastern establishment," though some of them retain a
positive image of the New Deal. Thus, whereas the elite defenders of the market contest anything that smacks of socialism, this other faction composed of communitarian populists
detests anything associated with liberalism.

Neoconservatism is therefore reducible to neither advocacy
of the free market nor right-wing populism, imperialist fantasies, or religious zealotry. It is predicated on the fusion of these
contradictory attitudes into a single amalgam that can serve as a
response to the two great political heirs of the Enlightenment[11]:
liberalism and socialism.[12] Combining an unqualified commitment to the market with xenophobic and religious zealotry would
give the neoconservative movement its ideological specificity.
The question was how to package the elites' interest in a free
market with the provincial temperament of a parochial constituency—or, to put it a different way, how to give government
back to the people and simultaneously cut essential programs
that serve the needs of the people. Selling this, indeed, was no
easy task: it took Ronald Reagan.

What sold best was brandishing a new image of big government working in favor of the welfare cheat, attacking a tax
system increasingly burdensome to everyday people, and adding a healthy dose of anticommunist nationalism peppered with

racism. The savings and loan scandals, which cost trillions of dollars, dwarfed the greatest ambitions of the welfare cheat but would essentially prove irrelevant. These scandals created only resignation about a system for which there was no alternative anyway. Social programs could become more affordable if different political priorities were set and the tax codes were revised in a progressive fashion, but that didn't matter. Such programs would only create new layers of "bureaucracy," waste, and abuse by those—with a wink—outside the white, religious, male community. Everyone knew what Irving Kristol had in mind when he quipped that a neoconservative is really "a liberal who has been mugged by reality."

Capitalism once again became equated with individual responsibility and the daring business entrepreneur. "Government," as Ronald Reagan liked to say, "was the problem." It was only the need to defend our way of life from enemies abroad that justified the myriad subsidies for the military-industrial complex. This was seen as unavoidable, insofar as the United States remained enmeshed not merely in a cold war with the Soviet Union but also in hot wars with movements for national self-determination. The original context thus emerged wherein the interests of business elites in eliminating "external costs" and pursuing imperialist designs conflated with the interests of a parochial constituency bent on recovering a sense of national pride and increasingly identifying the welfare state with the interests of the "other."

The victory of capitalism over communism created the need for nations to compete in what was becoming a genuinely global market; this meant streamlining production, trimming the fat, downsizing, and outsourcing. But the old enemy against whom our way of life needed defense had now disappeared. Once again, or so it seemed, the capitalist values of elites and the provincial concerns of the base were ready to clash. The glue was missing. And then came 9/11. The legitimate out-rage against a set of criminal terrorists directed by Osama bin Laden gave rise to yet another war and a new enemy: Saddam Hussein and Islamic fundamentalism. It didn't matter that Saddam was not a religious fundamentalist or that weapons of mass destruction were missing or even that he posed no genu-ine threat to the United States. Here was the "other" in a new guise, an unknown guise, which could easily be manipulated by a media fearful of being labeled "anti-American."

From the very beginning, however, major figures with roots in the regimes of Ronald Reagan and Bush the Elder were wary of pursuing a unilateral approach to the problem of Iraq. Various military officials saw the danger in stretching Ameri-can forces too thin. It was also clear to many that Islamic fun-damentalism could not serve as a substitute for the communism of old. But their position did not carry the day; it avoided the material interests and political imperatives of the new neoconservative enterprise. For them, 9/11 helped create a new context for linking imperialist ambitions and the quest for American hegemony abroad with hypernationalism and an even more intense assault on the welfare state at home. Thus, from the perspective of neoconservatives embedded within the Republican Party, this terrible event had the po-tential to reinvigorate the alliance between capitalist elites and "know-nothing" populists, along with their own power.

Ambitions

Even before the fall of the Berlin Wall, neoconservatives had been formulating policies whereby the United States might finally put an end to the trauma induced by the Vietnam War. The events of 9/11 provided them with the justification, once again, to exercise power in an uninhibited fashion. There is now no question that plans to invade Iraq had already been formulated under the regime of Bush the Elder by Richard Perle and Paul Wolfowitz. It has also become clear from the memoirs of Richard Clarke and others that, immediately upon hearing of the attack on 9/11, Bush the Younger became interested in the prospects for invasion. Terrorists bent on assuming "the worse the better" and long addicted to the romance associated with the "propaganda of the deed" would get what they wished, though, as usual, others would have to pay the price.

Inspired by a particularly vulgar form of realism, which has traditionally seen the state as the basic unit of political analysis, neoconservatives interpreted the actions of al Qaeda in terms of those enemies with which they were familiar, namely, fascism and communism. This enabled neoconservative policy makers to assume that the terrorists were sponsored by any number of rogue states that had to be dealt with forcefully rather than appeased.[13] The obvious need for a response to al Qaeda, which was accorded protection by the Taliban regime in Afghanistan, could thus be quickly transformed into the call for a more general confrontation with the "axis of evil"—Iran, Iraq, North Korea—and a new doctrine of the "preemptive strike." John Bolton, in fact, apparently told the Israeli paper *Ha'aretz* in February 2003 that the United States would "deal with" other members in the axis of evil once Iraq had been defeated. That none of these states actually had anything to do with al Qaeda, again, made little difference. As for international law, according to the *Guardian* (November, 20, 2003), Richard Perle told an audience in London that with regard to Iraq, "I think in this case international law stood in the way of doing the right thing."

"National security" has always served as an excellent slogan for equating the imperialist ambitions of elites with the interests of ordinary citizens. Making such a link has been turned into an art form by Israel, and the neoconservatives recognized that this little nation had much to teach. Israel had engaged in preemptive strikes against Libya, Iraq, Lebanon, and other neighboring countries long before the articulation of the Bush doctrine. And while constantly invoking its legitimacy as a state created by the United Nations, Israel has consistently flouted demands for a return to its pre-1967 borders and a host of measures concerned with the human rights of the Palestinians. Neoconservatives also saw the suicide bombings directed against Israeli civilians as anticipating the terror of 9/11 and the brutal, overwhelming responses in the occupied territories as a lesson for how the United States should deal with its enemies. These tactics were indeed carried over into Iraq by American forces: collective punishment of entire towns for individual acts of terror, the demolition of houses, political assassinations, mass arrests, torture, and the use of overwhelming force in response to demonstrations. Israel plays such an important role for neoconservatives because its most reactionary political expressions serve as a positive image for what America can become.

There should be no mistake. Zionism has never dominated the neoconservative worldview. Frank Gaffney, Jeanne Kirkpatrick, Michael Novak, and any number of leading neoconservatives are not even Jewish. They also recognize that Israel offers no real economic benefits to America or American capitalism. Israel became important to neoconservatives only after the Six-Day War of 1967, when it emerged as a military power in its own right. The interest of American neoconservatives in Israel has always been geopolitical. They see it as the outpost for American foreign policy in a region that is, in the words of Wolfowitz, "swimming in oil." Increasingly important for neoconservatives, however, is the way Israel serves as a cultural ally for the West. Indeed, many tend to forget about the influence of Christian Zionism and the institutional practitioners of what Edward Said termed "orientalism" on neoconservative elites and the formulation of American policy in the Middle East.

Neoconservatives are engaged in a cultural war against the "adversary culture" at home and anti-Western values abroad. Religious media, financial supporters, and the benedictions of Pat Robertson and other fundamentalist preachers for Ariel Sharon and Benjamin Netanyahu now suggest that even Jews are better allies than Arabs for the Far Right. Neoconservatives concerned with the "clash of civilizations" in the Middle East, including Samuel Huntington, are now growing worried about the Latino threat to the Anglo-Protestant identity of the United States.[14] They are watching carefully how the "wall of separation" being built by their erstwhile ally is helping to protect the Jewish character of the Israeli state from what Netanyahu has termed the rising "demographic threat" of Israeli-Arab birthrates. It seems that the point is never for Israel to fit into the cultural context of the region but rather for the region to accept Israel as its military hegemon and as a Western society. To ignore the use of Arab stereotypes in the "clash of civilizations" and that Palestinian control over the holy sites in Jerusalem and elsewhere might threaten Judeo-Christian civilization is to underestimate the need for neoconservatives to balance the geopolitical interests of elites with the parochial prejudices and cultural interests of a mass constituency.

Neoconservatives see the United States, like Israel, as standing essentially alone in a war against terror that, like the occupation of Palestine, has no end in sight. Ungrateful former allies in Europe that oppose intervention in Iraq have supposedly left us in the lurch; they are either too stupid or too malevolent to realize that we are fighting for them. It is the same with critics at home. Blinded by hatred of the United States, they cannot grasp that the enemy is stealthily preparing for another attack or that Hezbollah, Hamas, Indonesian rebels, al Qaeda, the Islamic Brotherhood, and the rest are all working together. The West is at risk, and dealing with that risk requires introducing into the United States what has already been introduced into Israel: an ideology capable of drawing—in the most radical fashion—the emotional distinction between "us" and "them."

Traditions

Neoconservatism seemed to be on the verge of crumbling before the 2004 election. The Iraqi war had turned into a nightmare, and its advocates were on the ropes. Establishmentarian conservatives in the business community bemoaned the costs, and among the populist Right, Pat Buchanan and others openly voiced their criticism. But the result of the election proved that there is a danger in being too sanguine. So long as neoconservatism is opposed only in piecemeal terms, or with an eye on this or that outrageous excess, its advocates will continue to set the economic, political, and cultural agenda. It is not merely a matter of contesting this policy or that piece of legislation, especially given the current cultural climate, but of beginning the arduous process of fashioning a different vision for the United States. Here it is possible to provide only a few cursory remarks on the nature of such an undertaking.

With respect to the economy, first of all, mainstream critics have avoided dealing with the way the inherently dynamic system of capitalist production erodes the community values cherished by populism. The secular character of capitalism, its obsession with technological progress, its commercialism, and its contempt for the parochial and provincial tend to undermine the conservative insistence on the importance of religious institutions, founding myths, and the received customs of the community. Neoconservatism is incapable of resolving this tension. The Left can intervene by asserting its traditional commitment to temper the whip of the market, highlight the concern for people over profits, and re-create a sense of solidarity and purpose in American life. The current conflict is, after all, not between big government and limited government but over what programs and priorities deserve primacy. The Left has a tradition on which it can rely in framing the choices facing the American people when it comes to government spending: it is the tradition of Theodore Roosevelt, the New Deal, and the poor people's movement.

The same can be said about foreign policy. America was respected by the world, or at least the Western democracies, when it stood for policies the world could support. It is absurd to talk about rejecting appeasement in a world war against terror when the rest of the world—and, perhaps even more importantly, world public opinion—understands the threat differently and is unwilling to support the self-serving and poorly formulated policy of a neoconservative American clique. Calling for realism in the struggle against authoritarianism means recognizing the constraints on building democracy: the suspicion of Western values generated by imperialism, the power of premodern institutions and customs, and the still fragile character of the state system in most of the world.

Our current neoconservative policy makers, intent on refashioning the world in line with their own fantasies of geopolitical advantage, are zealots. They have little in common with the genuine realists of times past. Churchill and Roosevelt in the 1930s did not blatantly lie to the international community about the threat of fascism, conjure up stories about weapons of mass destruction that did not exist, artificially construct a "coalition of the willing," endorse corrupt collaborationist regimes that lacked support from the populace, or employ violence without any sense of accountability; these were the tactics of their totalitarian enemies.

Then, too, there is the matter of civil liberties—the ultimate interest that "security" should protect. America gained respect in the world as a haven of freedom. It was the contempt for religious fanaticism, for the alliance between throne and altar, that differentiated the New World from the Old. Neoconservatives' insistence on constraining civil liberties in the name of security is, in fact, nothing more than the desire to shield their own incompetence and mendacity from public scrutiny. America has faced threats in the past; it is always easy to make the current danger into the most dangerous one. Civil liberties are easy to cherish under conditions of normalcy, but it is precisely under those conditions that they are least important. Civil liberties are not a luxury, as neoconservatives imply, but the foundation on which a free society remains free.

Neoconservatism is *not* coterminous with the Bush administration. Its sources have deep roots in American history, and should its sponsors suffer defeat in one election or another, like the rats in *The Plague* by Albert Camus, they will assuredly reappear down the road. Neoconservatism feeds on a peculiar set of public fears. It expresses the outlook of the provincial who fears what he doesn't know, who fears the criticism of established institutions, who fears the loss of privilege, who fears the eradication of outworn prejudices, who fears engaging the "other," and, ultimately, who fears freedom itself. The neoconservative is the closest relative that the fascist can have in a society wherein fascism has been discredited. Confronting neoconservatism thus involves more than simply judging a new philosophical outlook. It calls for making a decision about the type of politics that are acceptable, and unacceptable, in a modern democracy.

9

It Happened Here

The Bush Sweep, the Left, and the American Future

Political commentary is always replete with exaggerations; it fits the need of the culture industry. Even great thinkers like Karl Marx and Theodor Adorno tended to take the experience of a crucial historical moment and extrapolate its most dramatic implications into the future; it's a natural inclination. But the victory of George W. Bush in the presidential election of 2004 is pregnant with the most ominous economic, political, and ideological developments. The onus does not simply fall on "capital" in an election that cost nearly $4 billion and in which roughly the same amount of cash was spent on both sides. Enough elite sectors were suffering from a damaged economy and were appalled by the blatantly incompetent handling of the ill-fated and immoral invasion of Iraq. Republicans proved themselves masters of the smear campaign, and there was a question of ballot fraud in the two crucial swing states of Ohio and Florida.[1] But 2004 is not 2000.[2] President George Bush defeated Senator John Kerry (D-Mass.) by three and a half million votes, and the turnout reached a record high of nearly 60 percent. Not merely a plurality but, for the first time since 1988, when George Bush the Elder beat Michael Dukakis, a majority of American voters made a dramatic political choice. Staring into the abyss in the aftermath of a sweep that not only resulted in greater Republican control over Congress but also is being presented as a new right-wing ideological mandate, the Left must now look in the mirror and reflect on first principles. It must consider what strategy the Democratic Party employed, what the right-wing zealots are planning, what the role of the Left might be, and what outlines its resistance should take, considering that the country remains virtually as divided as it was in 2000.

Dealing with Differences

Could a different candidate have produced a better result? Perhaps, but probably not. Outside of Howard Dean, who would have received little support from the careerists within the Democratic Party, and whom the right-wing media would have shredded, none of the other candidates inspired much enthusiasm. Differences between the Republican and Democratic camps were also apparent, and in spite of a relentless and hideous right-wing media blitz against the challenger, the lying and incompetence of the Bush administration became public knowledge. But it is not that simple. The belief once existed that the Democratic Party—or at least minority segments of it—stood for certain basic progressive principles with respect to foreign policy as well as domestic reform. That belief was probably never fully warranted. The Democrats were the party of aggressive, liberal nationalism for most of the twentieth century. Now, however, it has become clear that if the party is to serve as an opposition, pressure must come from outside, or what might be termed "the street."

Whereas the Republican Party ran an explicitly ideological campaign predicated on mobilizing the base—by highlighting the threat posed to moral values, raising the specter of terrorism, wrapping the invasion of Iraq in the flag of national interest, and invoking the fear of higher taxes—the Democratic Party was guided by exactly the opposite strategy. It too, of course, wished to bring out its base. But its campaign was driven less by liberal principles, let alone socialist beliefs, as was claimed by various reactionary and religious demagogues in the Midwest and the South, than by the realism of the pollster and the pragmatism of the party professional. They believed that it was enough for John Kerry to appear as the anti–George Bush, just as, in the primaries, he had served as the anti–Howard Dean. It would seem from the results that the wise guys among the Democrats weren't as smart as they thought they were.

Asking whether a different candidate would have done better is actually the wrong question. More important is to reflect on whether *this* candidate left any kind of legacy that the Democrats might build on down the road. That is where the problem lies. Senator Kerry presented his party as a somewhat less noxious version of the Republicans and assumed a reactive, rather than a proactive, stance on the major issues of our time: social issues, the economy, nationalism, and the war. To his credit, Kerry did unequivocally state his support for *Roe v. Wade,* indicated that he would not appoint reactionary justices to the Supreme Court, and spoke about extending health care to the 43 million people who need it.[3] It should have been enough of a reason to vote for him. But elections are decided less by issues than by the mobilization of constituencies. Kerry said little about the declining conditions of the elderly poor, and he did not offer much more to those African Americans who would prove to be his most loyal supporters. Senator Kerry was also outflanked on the matter of gay marriage; he opposed the constitutional ban on it demanded by President Bush, only to watch in horror as Vice President Dick Cheney, surely to soften the hard-line stance of his boss, stated publicly that he didn't see the need for an amendment. The Democrats never articulated the vision of a nation steeped in tolerance and acceptance of the "other," a nation ready to meet the needs of social justice in an age of globalization.

As for the economy, Kerry was content to oppose tax cuts for the rich, but not for the middle class; oppose the outsourcing of jobs, but not put forward a plan for massive job creation; oppose privatizing the Social Security System, but not speak about raising benefits. Intent on developing "business-friendly policies," Democrats split the interests of working people from those of the "middle class" with incomes around $60,000. They also refused explicitly to accuse the Bush administration of engaging in class war, even though it had redistributed income upward from the poor to the rich more radically than at any time during the last century, constricted union political activity and the right to strike, and opposed raising an already pathetically low minimum wage. Too little was made of the fact that, for the first time during a war, programs for poor and working people were actually eliminated.

For the Democrats, it was always less a matter of challenging elites or reinvigorating the welfare state than engaging in what Bill Clinton liked to call "triangulation," which involves standing just a wee bit further to the left on economic issues than the Republicans. Kerry publicly evidenced the inner conflict of a man burdened with an exceptionally liberal voting record in the Senate and the "pragmatic" necessity of running against that record in the presidential election. During the last week of the campaign, he ultimately spoke less about the plummeting economy than the loss of 350 tons of munitions in Iraq due to the administration's incompetence.

What was true in terms of social issues and the economy became even more embarrassing in terms of dealing with the culture generated by 9/11. Much is made about the role of religion and the Democrats' inability to deal with the faithful, but actually, the number of voting evangelicals remained roughly what it had been in 2000; it was among nonregular churchgoers that President Bush increased his vote.[4] Most voters were concerned, especially in the swing states, with national security in the face of a terror attack and the conduct of the Iraqi war. Indeed, although religion and moral values surely played a role,[5] it was the inability to deal with the insecurities associated with the post-9/11 climate that sent the Democrats to defeat.

Throughout the campaign, Senator Kerry was effusive in his nationalism and his preoccupation with making the country more "secure." Rather than appear as the decorated veteran that he was, he sought to turn himself into a war hero. Kerry threatened to hunt down and kill Osama bin Laden and the rest of the terrorists with as much fervor as did President Bush. The only difference was that Kerry flip-flopped on his past as a resister during the Vietnam War, remained ambiguous on the Patriot Act, and unrealistically argued that the Iraqi occupation could be ended by sending in *more* troops, while maintaining that he could persuade the United Nations and our economically strapped former allies—whose citizens overwhelmingly opposed the invasion from the beginning—to provide help. The Democrats were simply not as convincing in their obsession with security, militarism, or nationalism as the Republicans were.

Maybe they were not quite as obsessed. This only makes sense because, right or wrong, the Democrats were considered the party of opposition, and they were supposed to offer an alternative. That was, after all, their rationale in the election of 2004. It was a rationale, however, that they neither fully embraced nor fully discarded. Senator Kerry criticized the set of lies that legitimated the invasion, but he never called on the United States to exit Iraq. Until the end of September, near the conclusion of the campaign, he said that he would have authorized the war even if he had known that Iraq was not harboring weapons of mass destruction. Kerry lambasted the president not for waging a useless and immoral war but for the incompetence with which it was being waged. This stance left him open to the charge of not believing in the legitimacy of the invasion while, simultaneously, engaging in Monday-morning quarterbacking. Kerry's catastrophic ambivalence on legislation calling for $87 billion to further finance the war, which he apparently supported but voted against anyway, was symbolic of his entire take on the conflict. That the invasion of Iraq was misguided from the beginning, *in principle and in practice,* never became part of the electoral debate, and for good reason: most of the Democrats, along with a new set of left-wing fellow travelers, took the bait and— especially when it looked like victory was near—fell over one another in expressing support for the Iraqi war. That the cheers turned to criticism once victory was no longer at hand seemed hypocritical, although, tactically and pragmatically, the shift in opinion only made sense.

Senator Kerry shied away from proposing a new approach to foreign policy or dealing with the need for a planetary politics in a planetary age.[6] The doctrine of "preemptive strike" was never subjected to criticism, and the loss of "the street" in so many nations—the squandering of sympathy and support for the United States stemming from 9/11—was never linked to the pursuit of a unilateral foreign policy instead of an explicitly multilateral one. Again and again, Kerry disclaimed the idea that any foreign nation or organization would hold a veto over American actions under his presidency. The problem, therefore, was not that the Democrats refused to embrace nationalism, fiscal responsibility, the feelings of the

Religious Right, or the war effort; it was that they did not do any of this with the same degree of *conviction and consistency* as their Republican opponents.

Advisers to Senator Kerry, such as Mary Beth Cahill and Bob Shrum, along with the mainstream associated with the Democratic Leadership Council, wanted to be pragmatic, realistic, and slick. They were. But the result was merely a watered-down version of the campaign they opposed. The contradictions and vacillations over foreign policy became ever more glaring. Although it supported Kerry, the *Economist* was not wrong when it claimed in its election issue that the presidential race involved a choice between "the incompetent and the incoherent." The real lesson of this election is not merely that the former appeared less noxious than the latter, which it did, but that the only hope for progressives—now irretrievably on the defensive—is to recognize that competence requires coherence and that progressive interests must be linked to progressive principles.

Republican Plans

President Bush actually put the matter well when he stated in his victory address that he had now earned some "political capital" and that he was willing to spend it. What is coming will be, if possible, an intensified version of what has been. The political trajectory for the administration over the next four years was set during the electoral campaign, and it will revolve less around what campaign strategist Karl Rove termed "mini-ball" issues than the "big" issues with respect to foreign and domestic policy. When seeking to understand this ideologically driven Republican Party, when constructing an image of neoconservatism, more is involved than discrete issues such as privatizing Social Security, eliminating taxes on inheritance and savings, introducing radical tax cuts, as well as repealing various environmental protection laws and other costs on capital. Such policies would undoubtedly increase the deficit. But man (and woman) does not live by bread alone. This would make it possible for the Republicans to justify eliminating state programs, but certainly not those concerned with national security or further bloating an omnivorous military budget.

Shrinking "big government" was never actually the aim of neoconservatives. Bush's deficit in 2004 was $413 billion and his military budget $419 billion. Roughly $4 billion per week will be spent covering the costs generated by U.S. involvement in Iraq and Afghanistan, and the cost of the partial privatization of Social Security could reach $146 billion by 2009. A $258 billion budget is projected for that year, without even considering the further costs of the war in Iraq.[7] The point is plain enough: only in terms of cutting *welfare programs*—often as "stealth issues"—were neoconservatives ever intent on, in their parlance, "starving the beast." They were always more than willing to expand the size of the military and the intelligence agencies.

"*Laissez-faire,*" wrote Kevin Phillips, "is a pretense."[8] The government *is* part of the economy; the real question involves the priorities it should set. Ideology is necessary in privileging one set of priorities over another. Viewing the state in terms of a family budget helps provide a basis for provincial thinking about fiscal responsibility, while the vision of an imperiled community, strengthened by the incessant terror alerts, creates the justification for building an ever-stronger military capable of enforcing a foreign policy consonant with imperialist aims. Those wishing to confront the Republican Party will thus have to deal with the connections it has forged among imperialism, militaristic nationalism, a new provincialism, and the waging of an economic class war.

Many now speak about the danger of American intervention spreading to Iran, Syria, and other states that are included, or might be included, in what President Bush called "the axis of evil." That phrase has been almost forgotten already, but it remains important for making sense of America's role in the world. More is involved than the particular flash points for potential crisis or even the seemingly unending attempt to read the present back into the original response to the attack of 9/11 and the assault on the Taliban. Generally ignored have been the basic nationalist and unilateralist assumptions underpinning the invasion of Iraq that were presented by Republicans—and are still being presented, now more than ever—as a line of demarcation between "us" and "them."

More than 56 percent of Americans now doubt whether the Iraqi war is worth the cost. That number is steadily rising, along with the dead and wounded. But the election of 2004 suggested that what is actually at stake is not Iraq but rather the self-understanding of the United States as *the* predominant world power with the God-given right to intervene where it will. Hard to ignore is the way the United States has lost the moral standing it acquired in the aftermath of 9/11. Republicans turned this in their favor. Former allies opposed to the Iraqi invasion and the international forum in which the Bush administration suffered its most embarrassing public setback, the United Nations, became targets of unrelenting criticism. The need for self-reflection by the United States and the need to develop new forms of Western unity were transformed into an unthinking nationalism, resentment against the rest of the world for its ingratitude, heightened preoccupation with security, and feelings of cultural superiority for leading the war against terrorism. The same hot air, the same propaganda, is now filling the trial balloons concerning the threats to our national security posed by Iran and Syria. Why not? Such talk helped the Republicans generate a *new provincialism* within the American polity.

The Democratic Party had no response to the wave of sentiments and attitudes reminiscent of the great character fashioned by Sinclair Lewis: Babbitt. The new provincialism reflects the overlapping consensus between the middle class and the depressed rural elements of American society. It exhibits not only a fear of criticism but also a fear of expanding individual choices and legitimating different lifestyles that challenge communitarian norms and religious strictures. It evokes the Bible thumping of the half-literate preacher, the attempt to introduce creationism as an alternative to evolution, and the thought that stem cell research and biological engineering will alter human nature.[9] The new provincialism is the neoconservative response to what Norman Podhoretz called the "adversary culture" of the 1960s. Grounded in moralism and disgust with abortion, gay marriage, and gun control, this parochial and reactionary ideology is ultimately intent on challenging the most basic elements of the progressive tradition: cosmopolitanism and tolerance, civil liberties and social reform, and, above all, the attempt to constrain the arbitrary exercise of institutional power.

Abortion was cleverly pitched in terms of a "culture of life" for the Republican base even while George W. Bush largely focused on "partial-birth abortions" in the presidential debates. But there is little doubt that the Bush administration will attempt to mitigate or even reverse *Roe v. Wade* with the appointment of possibly three new justices to the Supreme Court. The popularity of the new provincialism also provides justification for those who deeply resent abortion in principle and seek new conservative legislation. Newly elected senator David Vitner from Louisiana has called for banning abortion in all instances, while Tom Coburn, the newly elected senator from

Oklahoma, has actually suggested arresting doctors who perform abortions and trying them for murder should that procedure become illegal. Similarly, the newly elected senator from South Carolina, Jim De Mint, has made the modest proposal that neither gays nor unmarried pregnant women should teach in public schools.

As for gay marriage, it was a stroke of political brilliance for Republicans in eleven states to place gay marriage bans on the ballot; they were universally successful. But it remains an open question whether President Bush will fulfill his campaign promise of seeking a constitutional ban. The price would be very high. What is not an open issue, however, is the question of guns. Rather than take on the National Rifle Association, whose supporters would most likely vote Republican anyway, the Democratic Party simply concentrated on the importance of retaining the existing ban on AK-47s. Cries of "USA! USA!" directed against outsiders and unbelievers, however, did not vanish, and for good reason: the forest was missed for the trees. Ignored was the political role of ideology in favor of a narrow understanding of material interests.

Only by bringing ideology back in is it possible to glean hints of what will surely prove important for Democrats hoping to win the next election and for combating what must be understood as a more general distortion of democracy that pervades the American landscape. The Bush administration has already begun packing the lower courts with conservatives. Three new reactionary justices on the Supreme Court could have a devastating impact on civil liberties as well as on social issues such as abortion. Then there are the various "antiterror" intelligence bills, along with the Patriot Acts I and II. They give new powers to the federal government with respect to issuing subpoenas, denying bail to those accused of terrorism, instituting the death penalty for terrorist crimes, developing enhanced surveillance procedures, sealing off borders, and removing obstacles to investigating terrorism.

But the threat to democracy, no less than democracy itself, is not simply a formal matter. It is not merely the direct assault on civil liberties through legislation and various attempts at censorship that are crucial. Just as important are the spirit of intimidation and the self-censorship generated in what is becoming an ever more militaristic and provincial climate of opinion. The belief is growing stronger not only that the United States has been divinely endowed with the right to exert its power as it sees fit but also that intellectual activity is an affront to religious faith, that the political exercise of democratic rights is an impediment to national unity, and that the concern for economic justice involves an assault on the individual. Neoconservatives are bent on strengthening the military, waging imperialist wars abroad, and intensifying a class war against the least fortunate at home under the cover of a hypernationalism.[10] Cultural reactionaries and religious fanatics, advocates of the new provincialism, are intent on contesting the practice of liberty and the progress of knowledge. Support exists not for Nazism or for old-fashioned forms of racism and anti-Semitism but for a new American form of authoritarian populism.[11] That is bad enough.

What Now?

Not since Richard Nixon defeated Senator George McGovern (D-S.D.) in 1972 have the hopes of the Left been so thoroughly dashed. The greatest voting registration drive in American history, the most remarkable fund-raising effort ever, seems to have led to nothing for the Democrats. They were outmobilized by the Republicans. Even worse, evangelical fundamentalists and those threatened by the more liberal and cosmopolitan elements of modernity seem to have voted against their immediate economic interests and in favor of a radical redistribution of wealth upward, an old-fashioned class war directed against programs of benefit to working people and the poor, and a costly and unnecessary war in Iraq. The country seems to have been driven even further to the right, and it appears to stand more divided than ever before.

If the accompanying map has any validity, however, the present divide is not quite as new as it would seem. What becomes evident is a general division between rural areas threatened by modernity and urban areas intent on embracing it. This translates into a conflict between the classes and groups embedded in rural existence, with its religious and cultural traditionalism, and the classes and groups embedded in urban life, with its secularism and multicultural dynamism.

Interestingly, however, there is nothing new about that either.[12] Just as capitalists generally harbored an affinity for the free markets and civil liberties associated with classic liberalism, and workers historically identified with either Marxism or some form of social democratic thinking, the middle class sought refuge in the security of traditional values, while premodern groups, including farmers, small entrepreneurs, and the like, tended to identify with premodern ideologies. And they did so precisely because the modern world, both in its secular—liberal and socialist—theory and in its capitalist—industrial and technological—practice, is imperiling the existential and the material foundations of their premodern way of life.

Herein is the source of the new provincialism. Nostalgia for the power and glory of the American imperial past, which was questioned during the Vietnam War, inclines rural and premodern groups to embrace nationalist propaganda even in what is manifestly a failed cause. Fear of the outsider—in this

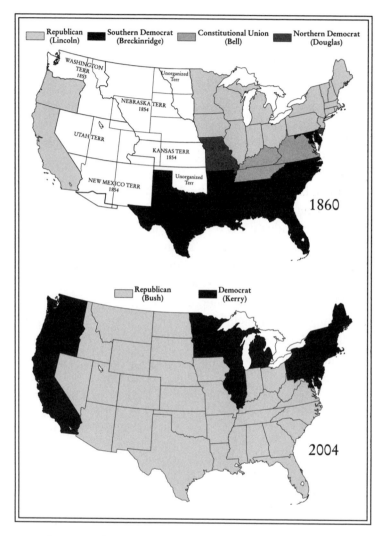

Note the map of states broken down into red and pink, blue and baby blue, counties in the website of CNN; http://www.cnn.com/ELECTION.2004/pages/results/president.

case, the Arab, not the Jew—similarly predisposes them to submit to appeals concerning security in the face of a looming terror attack. Ironically, if such an attack did occur, it would most likely take place not in some small town but in precisely the kind of major urban area whose citizens support the "left." Nevertheless, the new provincialism does not merely speak to issues of foreign and national security; it also bleeds into domestic concerns.

Most important, perhaps, is the rejection of a rights-based culture in favor of the "community." The decline in "family values" is bemoaned without the least sense of the way in which the "culture industry" is undermining them. The preoccupation with creationism as an alternative to evolution by the rural, religious parts of the citizenry complements their anxiety over complex scientific developments such as stem cell research.

All this reflects the deeper—perhaps unconscious—and totally legitimate insight that the small town is anachronistic in the modern world. Herein is the source of the oft-noted rage and resentment that these groups direct toward liberals and socialists.[13] The latter appear to be the cause of their distress, and this mistaken perception leads to contradictions; for example, the poorest counties in a state like Kansas vote Republican, citing religion and the like, even though Republican policies are doing nothing for them and are, in fact, keeping them poor. But simply citing the irrationality of such beliefs, even while calling for a new economic populism, misses the point. Privileging reason or utility in dealing with social problems is itself a function of modernity. This part of the citizenry may be voting against their material interests, but not their existential ones. Thus, when the question arises "what's the matter with Kansas?"[14] the answer is, nothing at all.

Political finesse ultimately does not help in dealing with this paradox. Something serious is at stake that becomes even more serious in periods of crisis, when religious (or mythical) and traditional (or reactionary) appeals generally assume heightened importance for precisely these groups. To be sure, in America during the 1930s, when they were offered something in terms of legislation that would *manifestly* better their lives, the faithful and the rural poor briefly aligned with the labor movement and urban immigrants.[15] The great divide was also bridged at other moments in American history. Consider the "new nationalism" of Teddy Roosevelt (R-N.Y.) or the elections of Democrats Woodrow Wilson, FDR, Harry Truman, and Lyndon Johnson. More recently, of course, there were the presidential victories of Governor Jimmy Carter (D-Ga.) and Governor Bill Clinton (D-Ark.).

But it is important to remember that these electoral successes were built on maintaining a racist political structure in the South and, perhaps with the exception of FDR, essentially employing a rank nationalism that brooked no opposition in the realm of foreign policy. Once President Johnson signed the Voting Rights Act of 1964 and mass opposition to the Vietnam War began—which resulted in a trauma born of the desire to render foreign policy decisions accountable to the citizenry—the "solid" South dutifully moved from the Democratic into the Republican column. It returned only when Jimmy Carter began the retreat from the achievements of 1968 and Bill Clinton, after running a smart campaign against George Bush the Elder in 1992, introduced his strategy of "triangulation" and welfare reform.

Such compromises, however, are no longer acceptable. Or, better, it is now the task of progressives to block the Democratic Party from entering into compromises that would sacrifice the interests of their base—people of color, women, unions, and the poor—in order for careerists and party professionals to get elected. Many, of course, see things differently. Mainstream

Democrats, who contributed so heavily to the ethical collapse of their party at the onset of the Iraqi war, are now already demanding that it shift even further toward the center in 2008. Given that the center has gradually inched further to the right since the 1990s, however, such a strategy will intensify the identity crisis of the Democratic Party. It can only further diminish its appeal for traditional constituencies and enable the Republican Party to fashion an even more reactionary politics. Such a strategy of appeasement will surely legitimate the antidemocratic and know-nothing elements of the new provincialism.

That doesn't seem to be a problem for noted *New York Times* columnist Nicholas Kristoff, who, in the wake of defeat, called on the Democratic Party to temper its support for abortion and gay rights and its battles in favor of gun control and against symbols such as the Confederate flag. But why stop there? Perhaps northern liberals can even be induced to buy pickup trucks, hang their guns and flags inside, and then drive those always willing people of color and poor women to the voting booths, where they can cast their ballots for the always deserving Democratic Party. But Kristoff is not alone. Another of the "great compromisers," paraphrasing Nietzsche, has an even better idea. Steven Waldman, editor in chief of *Beliefnet.com,* insists that Democrats should now empathize more deeply with how Christians—unlike the working poor or gay people or people of color, let alone Arab Americans—feel misunderstood and persecuted. It doesn't seem to matter that not all Christians, but only the religious zealots—the missionary advocates of the new provincialism—feel alienated from the Democratic Party. Perhaps those degenerate secularists on the coasts should start building a new coalition with them by insisting on reopening the Scopes trial.

Chipping away at the right-wing allegiances of premodern sectors in American society is possible, even necessary, but winning them over through talk of a new nationalism or a liberal nationalism that is contemptuous of multiculturalism and the achievements of the social movements is an illusion.[16] Obviously, points of common interest and even solidarity can bind the most divergent groups; perhaps progressives should support faith-based initiatives when it comes to the homeless, AIDS victims, and even prisoners, so long as it doesn't involve privileging a reactionary alternative to left-wing forms of community organizing. But it is equally obvious that conservatives can find reactionary ideological points of unity and fashion deep and sustainable alliances with reactionary constituencies more easily than progressives can. And conservatives need not qualify their support.

Dealing with premodern groups and classes, which the media like to define simply as "religious and rural" or "middle-class" voters, is, again, not simply a matter of political finesse. Snapping military salutes, wearing goose-hunting gear, and loudly identifying with religious values, as Senator Kerry did, won't do the trick. It evinces only condescension for small-town voters with strong religious and traditional values. They sense it, too. That is an important reason why the Republicans were successful this past election in identifying "religion" with the most reactionary elements of the religious community. As for the pragmatists and compromisers in the Democratic Party, those who have so little sympathy for ideological conviction, "red state" voters will correctly suspect that they are panderers and hypocrites.

Principled positions stated with conviction might actually sway some undecided voters. Fundamentalist groups do not represent the religious community of America. African Americans and Hispanics are both deeply religious constituencies: 89 percent of the former and 53 percent of the latter voted for the Democratic Party in 2004. Then there are the Quaker organizations such as the American Friends Service Committee, radical groups within the Catholic Church, and other religious institutions that were all once committed to building on the legacy of Martin Luther King, Jr. Most remain committed to fostering progressive domestic legislation and a humane foreign policy. Rather than speaking about compromising with religious fanatics or adherents of the new provincialism, it would be much more practical and principled for secular progressives to highlight their connections with the progressive elements of the religious community.

The purpose of parties is to get their candidates elected, but getting elected, especially over the long haul, often depends on the party acting as a vehicle for protest. That is the situation today. Economic divisions in the United States will become worse, a spiteful culture of intolerance will further harm the democratic discourse, and the domestic war on terror has no end in sight. The rush to the center, which will be presented as benefiting "us," not simply the party regulars, is precisely what will lead to papering over the gravity of these developments. It is what progressives must resist. Reinvigorating the Democratic Party is possible only by reinvigorating its base or, to put it another way, by providing core constituencies with proposals and ideals that working people, women, minorities, progressive religious institutions, the poor, and the young can be enthusiastic about.

President Bush and his followers promulgated an ideology concerned not merely with fostering imperialist ambitions but also with rolling back the policies and values associated with the most humane traditions of economic, political, and social reform. And ideology, as Max Weber reminds us, is not like a taxi that can be stopped at will. Might the Republicans veer even further to the right? Is that possible? It is, if we on the left let the obsession with security justify the constriction of civil liberties and a centralization of intelligence and police agencies. It is, if we let an arbitrarily defined axis of evil and the current contempt for international law go unquestioned. It is, if we forget about the lying and the distortion of democracy that have shaped the American landscape. It is, if we accept the right-wing identification of religion with fundamentalist zealotry. It is, if we don't link the war abroad with class war at home. It is, if we let a momentary mandate appear as a fundamental consensus. A new authoritarian populism is possible, in short, if progressives don't stand up to defend the values that have informed our best traditions: economic justice, political liberty, and cosmopolitanism.

Epilogue

Democracy, Foreign Policy, and War

September 11 was initially thought to have radically transformed politics. Old categories and ways of thinking about foreign policy seemingly lost their relevance. It became fashionable to speak of a "clash of civilizations," and suddenly, new forms of violence were apparently acceptable. Terrorism undertaken by suicide bombers, or what Ulrich Beck termed the "individualization of war," was thought to have supplanted battles between armies. Concrete interests, many believed, had given way before apocalyptic visions. The enemy was no longer a state but self-appointed representatives of a transnational movement inspired by fanatical religious beliefs. With the tragic deaths of 3,000 innocent individuals amid the collapsing World Trade Center, the difference between war and crime, internal and external security, suddenly seemed arbitrary. Even the distinction between war and peace had become fuzzy: everyone—everywhere—was now always at risk. The possibility of thinking rationally about foreign policy had seemingly been compromised.

All such claims of rupture now sound hysterical or exaggerated. Neither terrorism nor suicide bombing nor guerrilla war is anything new. Real battles have been waged from Kabul to Falluja. The state remains the locus for political analysis, even of transnational movements, and the Bush administration has already revised the "new" understanding of war by redefining the "war against terrorism" as a "war against tyranny." It has also become clear that most major terrorist acts directed against the United States, including the assault on the World Trade Center, have been inspired by hatred of the three traditional pillars of American foreign policy: support for the Saudi regime, support for Israeli policy toward Palestine, and imperialist intervention under the guise of human rights. As for the "clash of civilizations," even if the phrase could make sense of a world where fundamentalism and secularism are at odds in both the Occident and the Orient, it certainly was not unleashed by the attack of 9/11.

September 11 did not radically transform the character of political action. It is better to think of the event as a symbol of radical evil manipulated for political ends. The attack on American territory rehabilitated the fantasies of empire, emboldened the most reactionary elements of its polity, and endangered the best of its democracy. September 11 did not abolish the past but strengthened the worst American traditions. With the culture industry in the vanguard, buoyed by a spineless political opposition, the Bush administration transformed the legitimate response to a hideous crime into propaganda for the pursuit of an illegitimate and imperialist war policy. Most of its decision makers had the reputation of being "realists," while others, especially among the pundits and liberal fellow travelers, saw themselves as "idealists." But their thinking ultimately converged in support of the "preemptive strike," the invasion of Iraq, and a more explicit role for the United States as the policeman of the planet, the arbiter of terror, and the force opposed to the "axis of evil." Today, more than ever, a rational and radical approach to foreign policy has become necessary that projects a practical alternative strategy.

Manichaean claims reaching back to the Bible and the Koran, reconfigured and then carried over from the cold war, have been revivified by the new appeal of fundamentalist religion and rank provincialism.[1] But it is less a matter of abandoning realism and idealism—the two great intellectual traditions for thinking about foreign policy—than of noting how they have been perverted in the new context and what they contribute toward making sense of the modern world from a radical perspective. Striking is the unreflective character of this new realism, or "hyperrealism." Its advocates mouth the language of human rights, which became the justification of last resort for the Iraqi war, but they seem uninterested in more traditional pragmatic concerns: stability in the region, constraints and costs, clarity about the "national interest," and a precise definition of victory. Those seeking empire are more intent on reconstructing reality to justify their ambitions.

Genuine idealists rightly applaud the fall of the Taliban and Saddam, the elections that have taken place, and the new possibilities for the formation of strong democratic constituencies. But the elections are belied by the devastation wrought on Afghanistan and Iraq: drug lords still control the former, which is now among the poorest nations in the world, and a secular democratic consensus is still lacking in the latter. The claims of the Bush administration were phony from the beginning. The early promises to reconstruct Afghanistan have been betrayed. As for Iraq: there were no weapons of mass destruction, there was no alliance between Osama bin Laden and Saddam Hussein, the choice of enemy was arbitrary, and Iraq never presented a serious threat to the United States.[2] Good intentions were manipulated, and arbitrary power rather than discourse determined the outcome of policy discussions. The price paid by Iraqis for their democracy has been enormous: the infrastructure of Iraq has been destroyed, more than 100,000 people have been wounded or killed, and most of its major cities and its mosques have been reduced to rubble.

Amid the bloodshed and the debilitating prospect of an "endless" war on terror,[3] we need a new approach for thinking about foreign policy. The neoconservative vision is clear enough: a window of opportunity was opened by the fall of the Soviet Union, and before it closes with the rise of China and perhaps the resurgence of Europe, the new imperialists are intent on remapping the Middle East and turning it into the hub of empire. But resistance has marked the American pursuit of imperial fantasies. Like a spoiled child, unconcerned with what anyone else thinks, the United States has gotten into the habit of invading a nation, trashing it, and then leaving without cleaning up the mess. Huge demonstrations opposed the Iraqi war, and in contrast to Vietnam-era protests, they were genuinely international in character. The "street" confronted the Pentagon. Pacifist sentiments combined with a militant respect for international law, advocacy for human rights, and new demands for a multilateral foreign policy. Some on the activist Left have shown contempt for material interests, or at least for those who understand such interests in the most superficial sense, and their views have occasionally converged with more isolationist forms of thinking.[4] Leftist political professionals, by the same token, have often been too cynical about ideals and the role of ideology in politics. Revivifying the critical elements within realism and idealism would, in my opinion, provide a corrective for such deficiencies and a rough framework for a new, realistic perspective on foreign policy informed by democratic ideals.

Machiavelli's Revenge

Realism has usually been identified with establishmentarian interests. Its advocates view politics as not a science but an art. Different circumstances require different tactics. Always, however, its gains must be tangible. According to Sun Tzu, who wrote more than 2,000 years ago, politics requires a practiced and flexible hand; a "ruler who is unable to advance when he confronts the enemy is not righteous and one who looks upon the corpses of those killed in battle and mourns them is not benevolent."[5] In the same vein, by rejecting the calculus of power and closing their eyes to the concrete superiority enjoyed by their enemy, the Delians chose to die rather than submit to the Athenian invader during the Peloponnesian War: "justice is what is decided when equal forces are opposed," stated the Athenian representatives, "while possibilities are what superiors impose and the weak acquiesce to."[6] Justice can therefore be nothing else, according to Thrasymachus, the character most contemptuous of the critical ideals and the dialogic logic of Socrates in Plato's *Republic*, than the "right of the stronger."

The lessons taught by the early masters of realism are clear: success is the only criterion of judgment, power makes success possible, and those in power determine—according to their whims and interests—the norms of society. Or, to put it another way, power is the possession of the establishment, there are no privileged means, and realism provides the tools for avoiding conflict over ethical ends by the judicious use of force. Hence Machiavelli's famous justification for realism:

But my intention being to write something of use to those who understand, it appears to me more proper to go to the real truth of the matter than to its imagination; and many have imagined republics and principalities which have never been seen or known to exist in reality: for how we live is so far removed from how we ought to live, that he who abandons what is done for what ought to be done, will rather learn to bring about his own ruin than his preservation. A man who wishes to make a profession of goodness in everything must necessarily come to grief among so many who are not good. Therefore it is necessary for a prince, who wishes to maintain himself, to learn how not to be good, and to use this knowledge and not use it, according to the necessity of the case.[7]

Though *The Prince* would deeply influence the "great man" theory of history,[8] often producing a strange blend of the crude authoritarian and the romantic Renaissance adventurer, Machiavelli was never intent on having his prince conquer the world. He often warned against what we now call "over-reach," or the fantasies of empire, and he surely would have been bemused by the way the media's focus on Osama bin Laden and the bold act of his thugs has virtually obliterated any discussion of the Islamic world's legitimate grievances against the United States. Machiavelli's primary concern was more pedestrian than the glory of empire; it was for the ruler to stay in power and maximize that power. To achieve this required knowledge of the famous stratagems articulated in his works or the need to "divide and conquer," exploit human frailties, view all treaties and alliances as contingent, and always prepare for war while avoiding risks.

Relativism marks realism.[9] No "higher" principles can be brought to bear: God is no more on our side than Allah is on the side of bin Laden or the Iraqi insurgents. Religious and ethical judgments have little to add when it comes to evaluating the quality of political action.[10] Power is its own reward because it serves as the precondition for the satisfaction of material interests. Maintaining power no less than gaining it is the aim of politics. Acting from purely moral considerations is not merely naive but, given the danger posed by unethical political competitors, profoundly irresponsible. The ruler must therefore learn to drape his interests in ideals to secure the support of the masses; especially when developments have taken an unsatisfactory turn, such as in Iraq, this might extend to redefining "victory" by transforming the "war against terrorism" into the "war against tyranny."

With respect to elites both at home and abroad, however, it is different. The ruler may wish to exaggerate his power under some circumstances, but he must always render his interests calculable and concrete. The more calculable and concrete the interest, the easier it is to compromise; the less precise the interest, the more metaphysical and normative its definition, and the more difficult compromise becomes. The ruler must, putting it baldly, variously conceal and unveil the difference between the way things appear and the way they actually are. Ideology is never for him to believe, as the right-wing-dominated American media fully understand, but always for his opponents to believe.

Machiavelli was out of power when he wrote *The Prince* for Lorenzo de Medici. His lost his position as secretary of Florence when a Florentine citizen militia that he had organized was defeated by professional Spanish troops.[11] Machiavelli was banished to a beautiful house seven miles from his beloved city, and there he wrote his most famous tract in order to reenter the political stage. That work identified with the most historically progressive form of political organization in the historical context—the state—and it spoke, indirectly but insightfully, to the plight of Italy. Threatened by the burgeoning states of France, Spain, and Austria, its relatively autonomous principalities needed to be forged into a national entity, according to Machiavelli. The state, it should be noted, was just then coming on the historical scene. Neither as provincial and susceptible to corruption as the city-state nor as expansive and bureaucratically ungovernable as the empire, the state allowed for a meaningful monopoly of coercive forces, even as its justification—or what might be termed *raison d'etat*—became predicated on incarnating and defending what Hans Morgenthau termed the "national interest"[12] and on preventing the chaos generated by the masses entering public life or, in the worst instance, by civil war. Figures as diverse as James Madison, Metternich, Bismarck, Friedrich Meinecke, Max Weber, Antonio Gramsci, and others understood this. It explains why realism becomes popular, especially for elites, during the founding of states or when dealing with a genuine "legitimation crisis."[13]

In theory, realism privileges no particular form of government, but—especially in the *Discourses*—Machiavelli basically showed himself to be republican in his political views. He can be seen as yearning for a well-developed and confident citizenry capable of dispensing with strongman rule. But he distrusted any attempt to fragment authority. He called on the ruler to render himself autonomous, unaccountable, and independent even of those who brought him to power. How Machiavelli would have felt about manipulating the "national interest" and engaging in an uncertain war for uncertain reasons, however, remains an open question. *The Prince* opposed political experimentation for its own sake, recognized the difficulties faced by the reformer, and famously warned that "all armed prophets have conquered and unarmed ones [have] failed: for besides what has been already said, the character of people varies, and it is easy to persuade them of a thing but difficult to keep them in that persuasion."[14] Maintaining unity requires an enemy, and if such an enemy does not exist, then, obviously, he should be created. It is in this sense that the famous quip of Clausewitz should be inverted to read: "politics is war by other means." That lesson was indeed learned by the totalitarians, to both their immediate benefit and their ultimate detriment.

Machiavelli never regained power. *The Prince* wound up on the church index of banned books, totalitarians employed his ruthless instrumentalism, and his thinking became known for its amoral perspective. The amoral character of Machiavelli's approach to politics was not unique, however; that had been a mainstay of realist thinking from the beginning. It was the same with his claim that the most humane ideas can be employed for inhumane ends, and vice versa. Machiavelli's revenge rests on something else. It derives from the fact that in spite of the conservative implications attendant on *raison d'etat*—the right of the state to preserve itself even against the will of its citizens in emergency situations—he never accepted the assumption (always embraced by ruling elites) that the interests of citizens somehow find uniform expression in the will of the leader or even the national interest. The state and the leader are not to be trusted.

Machiavelli recognized the ways in which interests— always the interests of the ruler—are masked. If the mask should fall, the only recourse is violence.[15] Thus, although the good state rests on good laws and good arms, good arms are ultimately decisive; it may be best to be both feared and loved, but if forced to choose, it is better to be feared than loved. The author of *The Prince* understood that the interests of the leaders are rarely those of the led, and he understood that if ideology is crucial for preserving what Gramsci termed "hegemony,"[16] exposing the interests masked by principles is the first step in contesting it. Or, put another way, the critical moment of his method inherently threatens the natural desire of rulers to exercise power in as arbitrary and unaccountable a manner as possible.

The skeptical element within realism makes it relevant for progressives. No less than Brecht, who asked his audience to reflect on "who built the pyramids," Machiavelli begs certain questions: Whose interests will be served by a political action? What are the costs? And what groups will bear them? Intentions play no role here. It simply does not matter whether the leadership was "misled" by intelligence agencies or purposefully manipulated the information provided by them. What *does* matter is that the United States was mistaken about the weapons of mass destruction, mistaken about the threat posed by Iraq, mistaken about the connection between Saddam and al Qaeda, mistaken about the reception its troops would receive, mistaken about the costs, mistaken about the number of troops required, and mistaken about the character of the peace. Making a realistic political assessment of the Iraqi war thus depends not merely on moral claims—though these have a distinct role to play—but also on the extent to which interests have been falsified and costs have not been successfully anticipated.

Realism is not a theory, properly speaking. Machiavelli had an egoistic understanding of human nature, and his various proverbs speak to it. Where ability *(virtu)* confronts chance *(fortuna),* however, there are no fixed rules or models to employ. Each situation is distinct, and the politician with the best knowledge of the context, the interests of the other, and existing variables—and the will to put his knowledge into action— has the best probability of success. Machiavelli's insistence that politics is a craft or an art, rather than a science, leaves only the specifics of the historical situation for the activist to engage. Other than for ideological purposes, it makes no sense to extrapolate the thinking of the cold war, let alone of the

1930s, to try to make sense of the new millennium. Realism serves as a reminder of the need for historical specificity; its critical usage militates against metaphysical thinking and reified attempts to transfer the categories and strategies of one period into another. What the Left can garner from a critical understanding of realism is not a normative framework, not the ethical terms by which knowledge should be employed, but what Paul Ricoeur called a "hermeneutics of suspicion," or, to put it another way, a standpoint skeptical of ruling elites and aware of the need for an innovative confrontation with an ever-changing historical reality.

"Cynicism is cheap wisdom, " Kurt Jacobsen and Alba Alexander rightly note, "but it is still a wisdom to reckon with."[17] Activists who choose to ignore the imperatives of realism in the name of "higher" goals do so at their peril. Its ability to illuminate hidden interests, explode self-serving justifications for action, and generate concern for costs and constraints is crucial for those involved in any form of politics. Condemning this kind of skeptical attitude creates only helplessness in the face of "facts on the ground." Critics have an obligation to be clear about their own motives, their own hidden interests, and the sacrifices they expect from their supporters. Aversion to realism makes this very difficult. There may be more to politics than "who gets what, when, where, and how"—using the phrase of Harold Lasswell—but no serious political theory can ignore that set of questions in the name of "ethics" and still claim to be "political." Only the most vulgar and rigid realism, however, can deny the ability of ideology to grip the masses. Without recognizing the need for normative criteria to judge belief systems and inform the judgment of events, realism necessarily becomes unrealistic. Its advocate is no better than the cynic who, according to Oscar Wilde, "knows the price of everything and the value of nothing."

Idealism and Resistance

Pacifism is perhaps the most radical contestation of the human condition. Its refusal to divide friend from enemy, its absolute respect for human life against the interests of the collectivity, and its privileging of reason over instinct and the restraint of power over its arbitrary exercise pit principle against reality. Pacifism is a theme for each of the great religions, and, arguably, it unifies what is best in them. The Old Testament insists, "Thou shalt not kill!"; the New Testament calls on the aggrieved to turn the other cheek; the Koran condemns the taking of life. It is the same with Buddha. "Blessed are the peacemakers" is always the message of God. But (there is always a "but") then there is the existence of evil in a profane world. The Old Testament rings with righteous slaughter, Jesus comes with the sword, and Islam allows for jihad. This is the recognition by the divine that war has served as the tried-and-true form of settling grievances since time immemorial. The idea of a "just war" is the compromise religion offers to history.

Seeking criteria for the legitimate exercise of violence, religion pits the exception of the just war against the rule of war—spurred by interest and egoism—as "politics by other means." Emerging while the Roman Empire was disintegrating and Catholicism had not yet become a doctrine, the radicalism of this undertaking by St. Augustine and later by St. Thomas Aquinas should not be underestimated. Many before them had insisted that morality must be maintained even in the most immoral circumstances. But there was something new about the Christian insistence that compassion and conscience should supplant the Roman and medieval ideals of glory and heroism. War could no longer be justified, according to Augustine and Aquinas, by economic interest or political ambition. It was legitimate only as the last resort; it must be the decision of duly constituted authorities, and it must evidence "right intention." A just war must also have the prospect of ending quickly, and with success, and it must be limited to situations in which the evil it engenders will not outweigh the evil that exists. Above all, besides the existence of just causes for war *(Jus Ad Bellem),* there is the just conduct of war *(Jus In Bello),* which suggests that not everything is permitted: torture, rape, and unnecessary killing cannot be condoned. If duly constituted authorities are responsible for deciding on war and for negotiating the ethical injunctions of religious life with the profanity of conflict, the individual must be willing to assert his or her conscience and not blindly follow every genocidal order.[18]

Augustine and Aquinas, admittedly, were concerned primarily about mitigating barbarism in wars between Christian communities. There is no notion of a public consensus in their work or the right to engage in public discussion over the war and its ends; those in authority make the decision to go to war and determine the morality of its conduct. But then, Augustine knew the famous claim by Cicero that "society is composed of mankind rather than states," and the universal moment of just-war thinking was fairly obvious from the beginning. It was a question of turning life into the highest purpose, even the life of one's enemies, and highlighting what Renaissance thinker Pico della Mirandola would call "the dignity of man." Later, during the beginning of the Enlightenment, Hugo Grotius and Samuel Pufendorff would reformulate these concerns in the universal language of international law. They emphasized the direct character of the threat faced by a nation, the specification of interests, and the use of only proportionate force in order to defend the interests of the state. Nevertheless, with the Enlightenment in full swing,[19] the abid-

ing emphasis on some "natural" form of international law became complemented by a new sensitivity to the "other"—a
new contempt not merely for warfare and torture but also for
the various parochial and religious dogmas justifying them—
and what might be termed a "cosmopolitan sensitivity."

Kant drew the most radical implications for this form of
argumentation. His thinking privileges the intention beyond
the interest or prospect of success that impelled an action.
His political writings also offer not the state, which was the
case in earlier just-war theory, but a world republic of feder-
ated states as the institutional referent for the acceptance of
the "other" and the ability of the cosmopolitan "to feel at home
everywhere." Most important, perhaps, his notion of "perpetual
peace" contests the notion that war—just or unjust—is the
natural condition of humanity; it provides a utopian hope with
its own anthropological roots, along with an absolute standard
by which all treaties should be judged. Kant knew, of course,
that actions in the world are inspired primarily by material
interests; he believed that the world republic, which alone
might adjudicate grievances between conflicting states, was
impractical and that "perpetual peace" was a regulatory ideal.

Only such an ideal, however, might subordinate "realism"
to critical scrutiny. Even lacking an international authority with
the means to enforce international law, or a constitution to
determine what matters fall under the auspices of such an
authority, the need for judgment remains a "practical" part of
politics. The lack of absolute authority enjoyed by states par-
ticipating in a conflict is precisely what generates the need for
the individual to exercise his or her conscience. There is a
moment, then, when the privilege of making war extends beyond those in power. Kant, like Marx, was adamant about the
need to abolish "secret diplomacy." Here is the crucial political contribution provided by just-war theory and ethical ideal-

ism. These forms of thinking force the elites who "make" war, in the name of interests that are national and necessary only insofar as *they* describe them, to submit their ambitions, plans, and intentions to validation within a public discourse. Without such a discourse, resistance to war becomes justified.

Interest in the theory of just war was reawakened by the simultaneous rise of terrorism and fundamentalism at the beginning of the new millennium. In the aftermath of 9/11, the most absolute form of action inspired by the most absolute form of belief seemed to require the most absolute form of ethical criticism: the commands of Allah demanded condemnation by the commands of Christ. New issues came to the forefront: When is the use of force legitimate? Does international law trump national interests? Is torture justified to prevent further devastation by terrorists? Whether the religiously inspired vision of just law or the idealist tradition can actually deal with these new questions, or even with more traditional matters, is an open question. Neither has ever been as unambiguous in its responses as many, especially on the Left, would care to believe.

Separating the causes of war from its conduct clearly creates a situation in which a just war can be fought unjustly, and vice versa. Self-defense can also serve as the justification not merely for contradicting international law or securing geopolitical advantage but also for engaging in an anticipatory or preemptive strike. In the ongoing Israeli-Palestinian conflict, "security" has been used by Israel to justify its refusal to withdraw to boundaries existing prior to 1967 and its engagement in little more than a landgrab while building a "wall of separation." Just-war theory's old concern that the decision on war be made by duly constituted authorities may serve as a critique of al Qaeda, but it says very little about support for democracy. Compromise with dictators in the name of democratic ends, whatever the possibilities of "blowback," is perfectly in order. Minimizing casualties remains a legitimate demand, to be sure. Anti-imperialist and anticolonial movements, however, obviously cannot be composed of professional soldiers. The nuclear bomb and other modern forms of bombing, by the same token, undermine old distinctions between soldier and citizen almost by definition. Then too, determining what is an appropriate amount of damage ultimately depends on who is making the judgment. The bombing of Hiroshima and Nagasaki was a high price to pay for ending World War II more quickly. New discussions of the suffering experienced by German civilians during that conflict, brought to public attention primarily by novelists such as W. G. Sebald and Günther Grass,[20] put a new twist on traditional understandings of the "victim." The just war is never just to the innocent civilians, whose numbers have massively increased since 1914, and it is perhaps better to speak of "more unjust" or "less unjust" wars rather than "just" or "unjust" wars. As for good intentions, peering into the heart of a leader is a difficult if not impossible task. It really becomes a matter of how to judge interests against one another, and that is lacking in the idealist tradition and among those who support the theory of just war.

Realism begins with the belief that the end justifies the means. But that claim was always built on sophistry, for it begs the question: what justifies the end? As Kant knew, there is only one answer: the means used to achieve it. That insight projects the demand that lies at the heart of idealism: leaders and movements must be judged on the extent to which their policies evidence if not an "absolute" then at least a "plausible" connection between ends and means. Only by introducing this demand—and perhaps understanding democracy as both the means and the end of progressive politics—is it possible to speak about a foreign policy that is open to more than abstract criticism, that is accountable, and that ultimately reflects humanitarian values in an "open society."

Toward a Democratic Understanding of Foreign Policy

History suggests that democracies do not make war against other democracies.[21] But that is not to say that democracies have not engaged in wars against weaker, less economically developed "enemies"—usually yellow, brown, or black—using their domestic commitment to human rights and democratic norms as a cover for furthering their national interests or the interests of their parasitic elites. The idea that a clear divide exists between "free societies" intent on peace and "fear societies" obsessed with war is simply idiotic.[22] Distinguishing among interest-laden acts in a secular world cannot be mechanically derived from categories of this sort. "Empire" is not the province of any particular political system, although the possibility of inhibiting imperialist policies is better in some political systems than in others. Such policies, moreover, can have a corrosive impact on the freedoms enjoyed in free societies, both in terms of the nationalistic and xenophobic attitudes they tend to unleash and in terms of the harm produced. For example, in the United States, the Pentagon has consumed about $15 trillion in public revenues since the end of World War II and left a dilapidated social infrastructure, decaying cities, and depleted government resources in its wake.[23] Foreign policy is, in short, bound together with domestic policies; imperialist policies tend to make the imperialist nation less free.

Any foreign policy that claims the mantle of democracy must have what Dick Howard called its "democratic dynamics" judged in terms of both ends and means. Democracy differentiates itself from all other political forms by subordinating not only individuals but also the state and its leaders to the liberal rule of law. This implies a basic commitment to constrain the arbitrary exercise of power. Any democratic understanding of foreign policy must, similarly, begin with that commitment. Just as citizens are subject to the liberal rule of law in domestic affairs, so must states subject themselves to the international rule of law. The usual argument is that there is no institution capable of impartially judging between participants in a conflict. But the truth is that—for all its obvious faults—the United Nations is such an institution, and the problem is not its lack of impartiality but its lack of financial and military independence to enforce its decisions. This is exploited and, ironically, turned into the object of moral critique: hegemonic states must keep international institutions weak, usually invoking such institutions' incompetence or their "hatred" of the West, precisely to keep themselves strong.

Any democratic understanding of foreign policy must rest on reciprocity. Vulgar realists may believe that hegemonic states need to obey only those laws and institutions they choose to obey and should be free to arbitrarily exercise their power, unencumbered, on the world stage with the greatest possible degree of autonomy. Democracy is not a system, however, in which citizens obey only those laws and institutions they feel like obeying. Democracy calls on citizens to obey "the law," and with respect to laws they don't like, they are free to attempt to change them in a public forum. It is the same in terms of planetary politics. To be sure, reciprocity involves moving from the purely legal or political into the substantive and economic realms of existence. Liberal norms will obviously appear abstract when the majority of the world's workers earn less than $1–2 per day, and a foreign policy concerned with fostering democratic dynamics must concern itself with foreign aid and shifts in capital from the North to the South. Preoccupation with the "economic," however, should not be carried too far; the political has its own integrity. It was unbecoming for a democratic regime like the United States to substitute a bribed and coerced "coalition of the willing" for an international consensus in order to justify its invasion of Iraq, just as it was unbecoming to reject the legitimacy of the World Court because its rulings might oppose an often disputed notion of what constitutes American national interest. Such a posture is predicated on the most blatant celebration of arbitrary power, or what Drucilla Cornell and Philip Green appropriately termed "sovereignty in one country."[24]

Universal values inform any democratic conception of foreign policy. This should be self-evident, but in fact, the claim has been contested. With the rise of a postmodern way of thinking that rejects all universal categories and absolute claims, new emphasis has been placed on the particular grievances of blacks, women, gays, and other unique groups. The radical claim is that this form of fragmentation, or "atomizing," of the universal discourse on human rights did not strengthen but rather splintered the movement and bankrupted its social capital.[25] Universal claims have been used to justify the most barbarous forms of imperialism and the most useless and self-serving foreign policy actions. In offering such justifications, however, universalism is manipulated for elite ends. For example, the "white man's burden" was used to justify imperialism and racism, but it stripped universalism of reciprocity. Universal norms are too often identified with parochial national interests, to the point where the "cosmopolitan sensibility" falls by the wayside.[26] Instructive in this regard is the way the American media constantly trumpet the number of American deaths but hardly ever mention the number of dead and the degree of devastation among the Iraqi populace, for whom the war is supposedly being fought. It was the same in Vietnam and the same in El Salvador.

A foreign policy with democratic intent must exhibit a cosmopolitan sensibility. A cosmopolitan sensibility evidences a willingness to step outside oneself, to question the crudest forms of self-interest, and to engage the "other" in a meaningful way. This takes us beyond the institutional and legal issues surrounding human rights, and that is important. Many thinkers with different politics have correctly criticized the liberal idea of human rights for its legalism, its obsession with procedure, its individualism, and its refusal to privilege any particular social good. Introducing the cosmopolitan sensibility confronts such criticisms by placing solidarity at the core of political action and giving a social content to human rights. It also suggests that a democratic foreign policy seeking to further human rights must rely on more than a purely philosophical or institutional perspective. The cosmopolitan sensibility always highlights the plight of individuals who bear the costs of action. A foreign policy infused with the cosmopolitan sensibility and democratic values can therefore make no compromise with slogans such as "collateral damage"; an arbitrarily determined preemptive strike; torture of any kind, let alone of the systematic variety; or the suspension of civil liberties for enemy prisoners.

Any democratic notion of foreign policy must privilege multilateral forms of action. Surely, opportunities to advance human rights should be seized whenever Western hegemonic nations confront repressive regimes.[27] But this opportunism does not offer a new democratic perspective on foreign policy. Humanitarian ends retain a plausible connection with humanitarian means only when the authority of the United Nations is brought into play and justification is provided by international law. Authoritarian abuses alone are insufficient to justify "regime change." Interference from the outside has traditionally tended to strengthen the internal cohesion of even the most wretched regime. And given the brutal character of so many regimes, using the inhumanity of a state as the sole criterion for intervention would produce a foreign policy based on pursuing the exact opposite of perpetual peace. Navigating the terrain between universal imperatives and particular needs or constraints is the key to a realistic form of idealism.[28] In a period marked by globalization and the emergence of a genuinely planetary politics, self-righteous dogmatism and unilateral missionary zeal have become even more dangerous and anachronistic.

Democratic foreign policy requires international democratic will formation on its behalf. Exigency has always been the excuse for suspending democratic procedures. In principle, however, exigency with respect to an intervention—even to suspend genocide—must be argued before the court of public opinion. Any genuinely democratic exercise in foreign policy must rest on a meaningful international consensus. Admittedly, the collective here is abstract. Most Americans consider most participants in that collective to be remote at best and dangerous at worst. But that does not change the way the rest of the world views the United States. Baldly lying before an international forum such as the United Nations— not to mention the American public—about the existence of weapons of mass destruction in Iraq, its threat to U.S. security, and its terrorist connections constituted a betrayal of democratic discourse. It was precisely the "secret" dialogue within the government between the presidency and various intelligence agencies that smothered the true estimates concerning appropriate troop levels, the degree of resistance, and the prospects for "success" in Iraq. The "truth" came out not merely when important figures blabbed to the media or when a cowardly opposition finally showed a minimum of resolve, but when mass demonstrations trumpeted the lack of consensus and new information technologies rendered elite machinations transparent.

A foreign policy is democratic insofar as its interests and intentions are transparent. In other words, foreign policy is democratic to the extent that it is a public enterprise. Keeping the Internet free, increasing computer literacy, and expanding the number of legitimate sources of information are crucial demands for rendering elites accountable in the information age. The artificial manipulation of democratic will formation through the use of misinformation, intimidation of the media, and outright repression of critics undermines rational discourse and enhances the arbitrary and unaccountable exercise of power. The exercise of civil liberties by nongovernmental organizations, the ability to question policy claims, and the capacity to mobilize against what elites always claim is a consensus in favor of their views are therefore not merely aggravating impediments to "efficient" policy formation but crucial elements in determining the degree to which any given foreign policy is clear in its purposes.

Mobilization of popular forces remains a prerequisite for constraining the actions of elites. Although pessimism abounds about democracy, it is precisely in the realm of foreign policy that the greatest strides have been made. American elites are still incapable of dealing with the Vietnam "trauma." Not simply the loss of a stupid and unnecessary war, or even the need for a national consensus in support of the war, but the aggressive demands of public opinion with respect to determining the conduct of a war created a precedent that has extended to the Iraqi conflict. Various interventions and wars have been undertaken since the fall of Saigon. In the wake of Vietnam, however, it has become more difficult for elites to engage in secret diplomacy and arbitrarily act as they wish. That is as it should be. Making the arbitrary determination of foreign policy more difficult for elites, while checking the enthusiasms of the mob, is the essential purpose of democratic foreign policy

Any foreign policy predicated on democratic norms must place limits on what is permissible. Reasonable justifications exist for the exercise of violence: self-defense, the immediate threat of attack, or the clear and present danger of genocide. Some leaders and regimes are more responsible in their reliance on violence than others; the historical record and what appear to be the intentions of leaders are important criteria in formulating a judgment on any given policy.[29] Even under the clearest circumstances, however, questions should immediately arise regarding the level of military power a state should deploy and the degree of violence its "democratic" citizenry would find acceptable. What Albert Camus in *The Rebel* termed the "principle of reasonable culpability" contests both the cynical realism that assumes that everything is permitted and the paralyzing absolutism that pacifism projects. It recognizes the need for political action even as it cautions that common decency and common sense are being violated when, for example, more tonnage is dropped on North Vietnam than on all of Europe during World War II or when an unnecessary target such as Dresden is leveled or when Hiroshima is obliterated in the name of military efficacy.

Defining what is unreasonable can be difficult, since the context for military action or terror is always shifting. But it is relatively easy to grasp the character of a progressive response to these phenomena. Arbitrary power and terror rely on a politics of emotion and propaganda, as well as forms of decision making that militate against transparency. Its advocates seek windows of opportunity for the pursuit of elite interests, without reference to the costs borne by nonelite groups. Support for a democratic foreign policy will wither in an environment unconcerned with the demonstration of palpable threats to the national interest, a belief in legal standards and international law, and the need to set limits on political action. Or, to put it another way, the pursuit of a democratic foreign policy requires a prior commitment to democratic norms. Subjecting foreign policy to an idealist critique therefore results in a kind of tautology. Ironically, however, that tautology expresses a realistic assessment of the terms under which a democratic foreign policy must be conceived.

Even a democratic foreign policy can offer no guarantee of success in every instance. Not every decision made by its advocates will prove correct or meet the progressive needs of the moment. Omniscience does not derive from the embrace of reciprocity and universalism, the international rule of law and multilateral action, or the principle of reasonable culpability and uninhibited forms of democratic will formation. Foreign policy must always deal with unique, nontestable, and nonreproducible opportunities and constraints on action in a specific historical context. No general schemes or strategies exist that are appropriate in every crisis. Under such circumstances, in a world driven by ambition and power, it is tempting to believe that the end justifies the means. But such realism closes its eyes to the human costs of political violence: great cities in shambles, houses destroyed, cultural treasures lost, hundreds of thousands dead, hundreds of thousands more crippled, the environment devastated, talents wasted, and resources squandered.

So, if the end really does justify the means, what justifies the end? As stated earlier, there is only one serious answer: the means used to achieve it. Securing an absolute connection between end and means is virtually impossible. But insisting on a plausible connection between them is a reasonable demand. Foreign policy must show a degree of coherence if it is to avoid becoming enmeshed in imperialist fantasies, reactionary ambitions, and the arbitrary exercise of power. A democratic perspective on foreign policy calls leaders into account, justifies public decision making, and legitimates participation by the citizenry. It engenders reflection on whether actions supposedly undertaken on our behalf are actually in accordance with our convictions. It is small wonder, then, that professionals have always considered it dangerous to think about foreign policy in normative, let alone democratic, terms. The reasons are fairly obvious: thinking about foreign policy in this way makes us skeptical about elite interests, cognizant of the costs that others must bear, and, ultimately, aware of what kind of people we are.

Notes

7. Dub'ya's Fellow Travelers

1. Note the responses in the *Nation* (November 29, 2004) to Anatol Lieven, "Liberal Hawk Down," *Nation* (October 25, 2004), 29–34, a stinging critique of a truly awful anthology, *The Fight Is for Democracy: Winning the War of Ideas in America and the World,* ed. George Packer (New York: Perennial, 2003), which highlights the ignorance and prejudices of Paul Berman and other prominent contributors when it comes to the Middle East.

2. Michael Walzer, "Can There Be a Decent Left?" *Dissent* 49, no. 2 (Spring 2002). A Hitchens article on September 28, 2001, suggested that journalist John Pilger and playwright Harold Pinter were inclined to express such glee. The next month, the *Guardian* apologized to both men, who suggested nothing of the sort.

3. Michael Tomasky, "Between Cheney and Chomsky: Making a Domestic Case for a New Liberal Foreign Policy," in *The Fight Is for Democracy*, 21ff.

4. Adam Shatz, "The Left and 9/11," *Nation* (September 23, 2002), and the searing response by Lawrence McGuire, "Eight Ways to Smear Noam Chomsky," *Counterpunch* (October 9, 2002).

5. Todd Gitlin, "Varieties of Patriotic Experience," in *The Fight Is for Democracy*, 109, 110, 126.

6. Susie Linfield, "The Treason of the Intellectuals (Again)," in *The Fight Is for Democracy*, 166.

7. The manifesto has been published as the appendix to Jean Bethke Elshtain, *Just War against Terror: The Burden of American Power in a Violent World* (New York: Basic Books, 2003), 182–207.

8. Ibid.,1ff.

9. Michael Walzer, "Justice and Injustice in the Gulf War," in *But Was*

It Just? Reflections on the Morality of the Persian Gulf War, ed. David E. Decosse (New York: Doubleday, 1992), 1ff. Jean Bethke Elshtain, "Just War as Politics: What the Gulf War Told Us about Contemporary American Life," in ibid., 43ff., she never explicitly takes a position but warns us against triumphalism and cautions that judging the conflict is "complex."

10. Because he was defending an authoritarian and aggressive regime, "Saddam's war is unjust, even though he didn't start the fighting." By the same token, since other "measures short of full-scale war were possible . . . America's war is [also] unjust." What to do? "Now that we are fighting [the war], I hope that we win it and the Iraqi regime collapses quickly. I will not march to stop the war while Saddam is still standing." Michael Walzer, *Arguing War* (New Haven, Conn.: Yale University Press, 2004), 160–61.

11. Ibid., 162–68.

12. Clarity is achieved, or so Walzer believes, once a sense of tradition and community is introduced. That will apparently help in interpreting the degree of peril posed by the situation, since "the license of supreme emergency can only be claimed by political leaders whose people have already risked everything and who know how much they have at risk." Ibid., 44.

13. Ibid. 138–42. See Ori Lev's review of Walzer's *Arguing for War* in *Logos* 3, no. 4 (Fall 2004).

14. This is the condensed version of an article that appeared in the winter 2003 issue of *Dissent.* It originally appeared in an on-line symposium entitled "Writers, Artists, and Civic Leaders on the War," sponsored by OpenDemocracy.net.

15. UN bashing is mostly disingenuous or ignorant. There is usually little that the UN can do independently of the Security Council, where the United States wields its veto and its overwhelming influence. See the fine account by Linda Polman, *We Did Nothing: Why the Truth Does Not Always Go Out When the UN Goes In* (London: Viking, 2003).

16. See chapter 3 of this volume.

17. See the four issues of *Logos* constituting vol. 2 (2003).

18. Michael Lind, *Vietnam: The Necessary War: A Reinterpretation of America's Most Disastrous Conflict* (New York: Free Press, 2002).

19. See chapter 1 of this volume.

20. Christopher Hitchens, *Unacknowledged Legislation: Writer in the Public Sphere* (London: Verso, 2000), 102, 105.

21. Christopher Hitchens, "Goodbye to Berlin," in *Unacknowledged Legislation,* 138–39.

22. Michael Ignatieff, *The Lesser Evil: Political Ethics in an Age of Terror* (Princeton, N.J.: Princeton University Press, 2003).

23. Michael Ignatieff, "The Year of Living Dangerously: A Liberal Supporter of the War Looks Back," *New York Times Magazine* (March 14, 2004).

24. Of his anti–Vietnam War days, marching with distasteful pacifists, Ignatieff says, "Since I was anti-communist, I actually had more in common with the liberal hawks who thought they were defending South Vietnam against advancing communist tyranny. But I believed that nothing could save the weak and corrupt South Vietnamese government." See his "Friends Disunited," *Guardian* (March 24, 2003). The ethical argument here is lame, to put it mildly.

25. Michael Ignatieff, "The American Empire (Get Used to It)," *New York Times Magazine* (January 5, 2003).

26. Michael Ignatieff, *Empire Lite* (New York: Minerva, 2003), 23. See Michael Neuman's scorching essay "The Apostle of He-manitarianism," *Counterpunch* (December 8, 2003), www.counterpunch.org/neumann 12082003.html.

27. Paul Berman, *Terror and Liberalism* (New York: Norton, 2002), 192.

28. The casualty figures too are a source of controversy. Even by "lowball" estimates, the toll is shocking. See, for example, www.iraqbodycount.net. On the dubious use of numbers from the start, see, for example, David Walsh, "Washington Conceals US Casualties in Iraq" (February 4, 2004), http://www.wsws.org/articles/2004/feb2004/woun-f04.shtml.

8. Constructing Neoconservatism

1. David Frum and Richard Perle, *An End to Evil: How to Win the War on Terror* (New York: Random House, 2004).

2. John Ehrenberg, "The Committee's Project: From SALT to Baghdad," *Logos* 3, no. 2 (Spring 2004).

3. Michael Oakeshott, *Rationalism in Politics and Other Essays* (Indianapolis: Liberty Fund, 1991).

4. Anne Norton, *Leo Strauss and the Politics of American Empire* (New Haven, Conn.: Yale University Press, 2004). See also the intelligent articles by Mark Lilla, "The Closing of the Straussian Mind," *New York Review of Books* (November 4, 2004), 55ff., and Nick Xenos, "Leo Strauss and the Rhetoric of the War on Terror," *Logos* 3, no. 2 (Spring 2004).

5. Fear of nihilism and relativism and contempt for the splitting of politics from religion and classical ethics, all of which becomes apparent in Machiavelli, lie behind the seminal work of Leo Strauss, *Natural Right and History* (Chicago: University of Chicago Press, 1965).

6. Robert Kagan, *Of Paradise and Power: America and Europe in the New World Order* (New York: Knopf, 2003).

7. Michael A. Ledeen, *The War against the Terror Masters: Why It Happened, Where We Are Now, How We'll Win* (New York: St. Martin's, 2003); Charles Murray, *Losing Ground: American Social Policy 1950–1980* (New York: Basic Books, 1995).

8. Norman Podhoretz, *The Bloody Crossroads: Where Literature and Politics Meet* (New York: Holiday House, 1986); also see my review in the *Texas Observer* (December 19, 1986).

9. Milton Friedman, *Capitalism and Freedom* (Chicago: University of Chicago Press, 2002); F. A. Hayek, *The Road to Serfdom* (Chicago: University of Chicago Press, 1994); Robert Nozick, *Anarchy, State, Utopia* (New York: Basic Books, 1977).

10. Chip Berlet and Matthew N. Lyon, *Right Wing Populism in America* (New York: Guilford Press, 2000).

11. Note the attempt to view the Enlightenment as the foundation for "compassionate conservatism," by eliminating its most radical trends, by Gertrude Himmelfarb, *The Roads to Modernity: The British, French, and American Enlightenments* (New York: Knopf, 2004), and my review, "Neo-Cons and Philosophes," *Washington Post* (September 12, 2004).

12. Stephen Eric Bronner, *Reclaiming the Enlightenment: Toward a Politics of Radical Engagement* (New York: Columbia University Press, 2004).

13. For a somewhat different perspective on the rogue state, see Clyde Prestowitz, *Rogue Nation: American Unilateralism and the Failure of Good Intentions* (New York: Basic Books, 2003).

14. Samuel Huntington, *The Clash of Civilizations and the Remaking of World Order* (New York: Simon and Schuster, 1998), and *Who Are We: The Challenge to America's National Identity* (New York: Simon and Schuster, 2004).

9. It Happened Here

1. See the fine article by Kurt Jacobsen, "Tin Foil Hats, the MSM and Election Mischief," *Logos* 4, no. 1 (Winter 2005).

2. Douglas Kellner, *Grand Theft 2000: Media Spectacle and a Stolen Election* (Lanham, Md.: Rowman and Littlefield, 2001).

3. "The number of people with health insurance rose by 1.5 million between 2001 and 2002, to 242.4 million, and the number of uninsured rose by 2.4 million, to 43.6 million, the U.S. Census Bureau reported today. An estimated 15.2 percent of the population had no health insurance coverage during all of 2002, up from 14.6 percent in 2001, according to the report, Health Insurance Coverage in the United States: 2002. The proportion of insured children did not change in 2002, remaining at 64.8 mil-

lion, or 88.4 percent of all children." The situation has only gotten worse since these figures were published in *U.S. Department of Commerce News* (September 30, 2003). For the full report, see www.census.gov/Press-Release/www/2003/cb03–154.html.

4. www.washingtonpost.com/wp-dyn/articles/A31003–2004Nov6_2.html.

5. A Zogby poll conducted for the Catholic peace group Pax Christi, the New York–based civic advocacy group Res Publica, and the Center for American Progress found that 42 percent of voters cited the war in Iraq as *the* most pressing moral issue, and 31 percent cited poverty and economic justice; only 13 percent cited abortion, and 9 percent cited same-sex marriage. See www.washingtonpost.com/ac2/wp-dyn/A38001–2004Nov92.html.

6. See the anthology *Planetary Politics: Human Rights, Terror, and Global Society,* ed. Stephen Eric Bronner (Lanham, Md.: Rowman and Littlefield, 2005).

7. Jonathan Wiesman, "Analysts Call Outlook for Bush Plan Bleak: Too Much Deficit, Not Enough Revenue," www.washingtonpost.com, November 5, 2004, A08.

8. Kevin Phillips, *Wealth and Democracy: A Political History of the American Rich* (New York: Broadway, 2003).

9. Such primitive fears are given sophisticated forms in Francis Fukuyama, *Our Posthuman Future: Consequences of the Biotechnology Revolution* (New York: Picador, 2002).

10. Frances Fox Piven, *The War at Home: The Domestic Costs of Bush's Militarism* (New York: New Press, 2004).

11. When Sinclair Lewis wrote *It Can't Happen Here* (1935), which dealt with a fascist takeover of America, that movement, with its anti-Semitism, was a salient reality and international in its appeal. By contrast, exaggerating reactionary possibilities, manipulating the frisson of Nazism through continuing references to the 1930s, and employing the old anti-Semitism in new conditions both misrepresents the primary potential victims and distorts the real threat of the present. See the vastly overpraised novel by Philip Roth, *The Plot against America* (New York: Houghton Mifflin, 2004).

12. Karl Marx, "The Eighteenth Brumaire of Louis Bonaparte," in Karl Marx and Frederick Engels, *Selected Works,* 3 vols. (Moscow: Progress Publishers, 1969), 1:394ff.

13. Premodern class formations have traditionally served as the mass base for fascism in Europe and for other right-wing authoritarian movements in the United States, such as the Ku Klux Klan. The classic analysis is by Ernst Bloch, *Heritage of Our Times,* trans. Neville and Stephen Plaice (Berkeley: University of California Press, 1991), 97–148.

14. Thomas Frank, *What's the Matter with Kansas? How Conservatives Won the Heart of America* (New York: Metropolitan Books, 2004).

15. Instructive in this regard is the preacher Jim Casey in *The Grapes of Wrath* by John Steinbeck. See the Internet article by Mark Solomon, "What's Next? Let's Build 'The Mother of All Coalitions,'" moderator@portside.org (November 12, 2004).

16. Michael Lind, *The Next American Nation: The New Nationalism and the Fourth American Revolution* (New York: Free Press, 1996), and *Up from Conservatism: Why the Right Is Wrong from America* (New York: Free Press, 1997). Not merely a less opportunistic but also a more coherent position is offered by Charles Noble, *The Collapse of Liberalism: Why America Needs a New Left* (Lanham, Md.: Rowman and Littlefield, 2004).

Epilogue

1. "The strength of terrorism lies in its ability to translate human and social phenomena into religious language: justice becomes the Good; wrong becomes Evil; the political adversary becomes the infidel." Nadia Urbanati, "Terror and Politics," in *Planetary Politics: Human Rights, Terror, and Global Society,* ed. Stephen Eric Bronner (Lanham, Md.: Rowman and Littlefield, 2005), 65.

2 .Scott Ritter, *Frontier Justice: Weapons of Mass Destruction and the Bushwhacking of America* (New York: Context Books, 2003).

3. Carl Boggs, *Imperial Delusions: American Militarism and Endless War* (Lanham, Md.: Rowman and Littlefield, 2005).

4. Note the interview with Jude Wanniski, a former associate editor of the *Wall Street Journal* and economic adviser to the Reagan administration, and the article by Patrick J. Buchanan, "Whose War?" in the huge anthology of otherwise mostly left-leaning Catholics entitled *Neo-Conned: Hypocrisy, Lawlessness, and the Rape of Iraq* (Vienna, Va.: HIS Press, 2005).

5. Sun Tzu, *The Art of War,* trans. Samuel B. Griffith (New York: Oxford University Press, 1963), 151.

6. Thucydides, *The Peloponnesian War,* trans. Steven Lattimore (Indianapolis: Hackett, 1998), 295.

7. Niccolo Machiavelli, "The Prince," in *The Prince and the Discourses* (New York: Modern Library, 1950), 56.

8. See the collection of essays by Thomas Carlyle, *On Heroes, Hero-Worship, and the Heroic in History* (Omaha: University of Nebraska Press, 1966).

9. "Whence it may be seen that hatred is gained as much by good work as by evil, and therefore, as I said before, a prince who wishes to maintain the state is often forced to do evil." Machiavelli, *The Prince,* 71.

10. Note the classic essay by Max Weber, "Politics as a Vocation," in *From Max Weber: Essays in Sociology,* ed. H. H. Gerth and C. W. Mills (New York: Oxford University Press, 1946), 77ff.

11. He was a staunch supporter of the state employing a popular militia rather than foreign mercenaries, unconcerned with burgeoning developments in international law, and insistent on victory at any price by strategically flexible and innovative commanders. A military perspective akin to the notion of conventional politics emerged in Niccolo Machiavelli, *The Art of War,* trans. Ellis Farnesworth (Indianapolis: Bobbs Merrill, 1965).

12. Hans J. Morgenthau, *Politics among Nations: The Struggle for Power and Peace* (New York: Knopf, 1985), 451–61, 526–33.

13. Jürgen Habermas, *Legitimation Crisis,* trans. Thomas McCarthy (Boston: Beacon, 1975).

14. Machiavelli, *The Prince,* 22.

15. "Thus it is well to seem merciful, faithful, humane, sincere, religious, and also to be so; but you must have the mind so disposed that when it is needful to be otherwise you may be able to change to the opposite qualities." Machiavelli, *The Prince,* 65.

16. Antonio Gramsci, *Selections from the Prison Notebooks,* ed. Quintin Hoare and Geoffrey Nowell Smith (New York: International Publishers, 1971), 245ff. and passim.

17. Kurt Jacobsen and Alba Alexander, "Playing the Angel's Advocate: Human Rights, Global Realism, and the Politics of Intervention," in *Planetary Politics,* 200.

18. Note the fine work by Seymour Hersh, *Chain of Command: The Road from 9/11 to Abu Ghraib* (New York: HarperCollins, 2004).

19. For a fuller elaboration, see Stephen Eric Bronner, *Reclaiming the Enlightenment: Towards a Politics of Radical Engagement* (New York: Columbia University Press, 2004).

20. W. G. Sebald, *On the Natural History of Destruction,* trans. Anthea Bell (New York: Random House, 2003); Günther Grass, *Crabwalk* (New York: Harcourt, 2003).

21. Charles Lipson, *Reliable Partners: How Democracies Have Made a Separate Peace* (Princeton, N.J.: Princeton University Press, 2004).

22. Cf. Natan Sharansky and Ron Dermer, *The Case for Democracy: The Power of Freedom to Overcome Tyranny and Terror* (New York: Public Affairs Press, 2004).

23. Carl Boggs, "The New Militarism: Imperial Overreach," in *Planetary Politics,* 83.

24. Drucilla Cornell and Philip Green, "Multilateralism: For a New Political Enlightenment," in *Planetary Politics,* 139.

25. Micheline Ishay, *The History of Human Rights: From Ancient Times to the Globalization Era* (Berkeley: University of California Press, 2004), 316ff. and passim.

26. Stephen Eric Bronner, *Ideas in Action: Political Tradition in the Twentieth Century* (Lanham, Md.: Rowman and Littlefield, 1999), 329ff.

27. Micheline Ishay, "Human Rights in the Age of Empire," in *Planetary Politics,* 213.

28. See the excellent study by Carol C. Gould, *Globalizing Democracy and Human Rights* (New York: Cambridge, 2004).

29. Philip Green and Drucilla Cornell, "The Prospect before Us; Second Thoughts on Humanitarian Intervention," *Logos* 3, no. 4 (Fall 2004).

Index